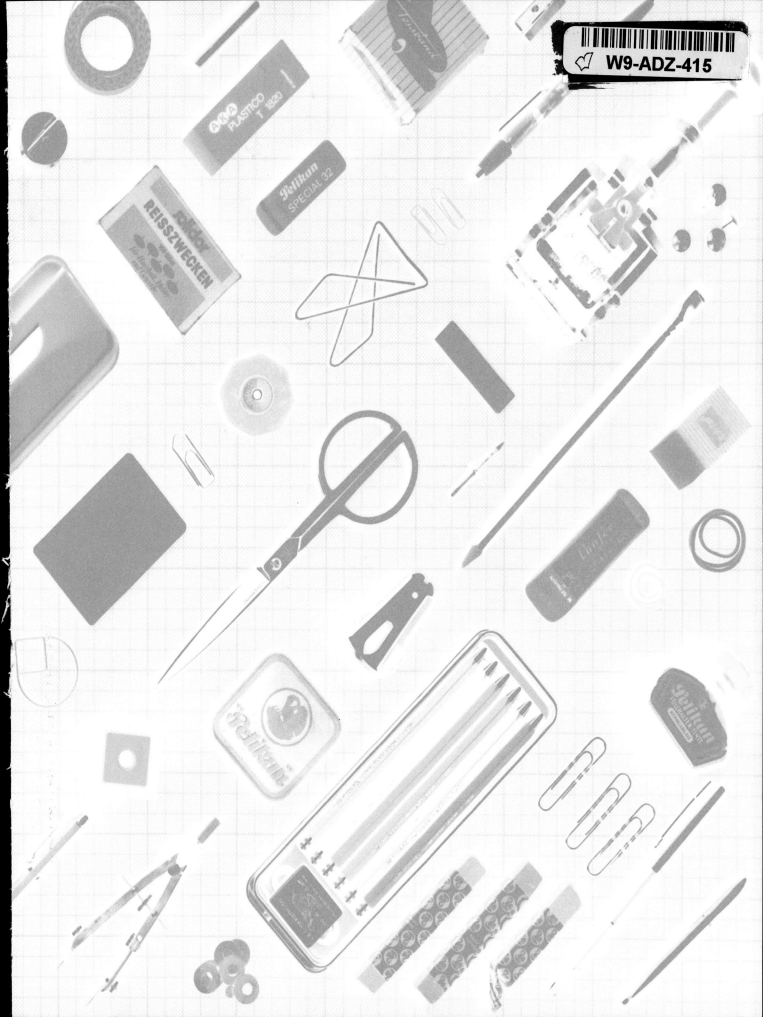

STATIONERY FEVER

STATIONERY FEVER

From Paper Clips to Pencils and Everything in Between

written by
John Z. Komurki

edited by
Angela Nicoletti
Luca Bendandi

PRESTEL

Munich • London • New York

Contents

INTRO   6

CHAPTER Nº 1
PENCIL   8

Blackwing 602   22
CW Pencil Enterprise   24
Giulio Iacchetti   30
The Erasable Podcast   34
R.S.V.P.   38

CHAPTER Nº 2
SHARPENER   44

The Grenade   51
David Rees   52
Nakajima Jukyudo   56
Inkwell Berlin   60
Papier Tigre   66

CHAPTER Nº 3
ERASER   70

Pink Pearl   74
Choosing Keeping   80
McNally Jackson   86

CHAPTER Nº4
PEN   92

Parker 51   99
Space Pen   102
Pen Store   104
Present & Correct   108

CHAPTER Nº5
NOTEBOOK   114

Moleskine   122
Faber   124
Publicações Serrote   128
Papelote   134

CHAPTER Nº6
GLUE   140

Coccoina   145
MT Masking Tape   146

CHAPTER Nº7
POST   150

Bonvini   158
Tampographe Sardon   164

CHAPTER Nº8
SCHOOL   168

Crayola   173
Museo del Quaderno   178
Kakimori   180
Rad and Hungry   184

CHAPTER Nº9
OFFICE   190

Zenith 548   195
Daphna Laurens   202

CREDITS   206

Photo Credits
Further Reading
Acknowledgements

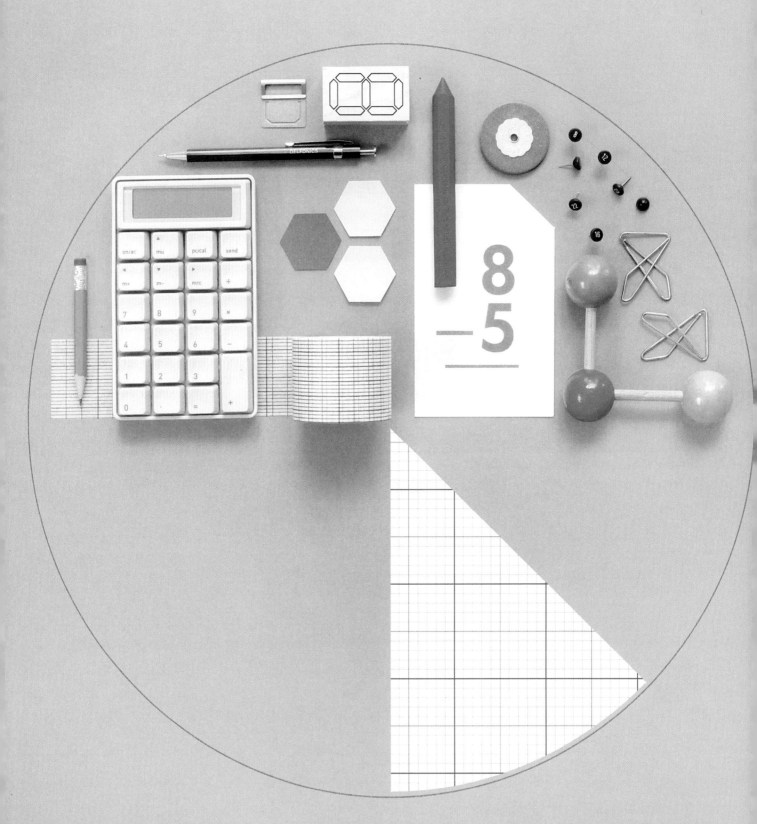

INTRO

Stationery is undergoing a worldwide renaissance. Partly in defiance of digital media, beautifully-designed objects from the past and present are once again appearing on desks as tools, as ornaments and as status symbols. There is a growing movement of people who are turning away from the homogenous patina of the digitally-created and experimenting with pen and ink and pencil and paper, and rediscovering the processes these materials give rise to.

Stationery Fever provides a panoramic overview of this cultural development. Collectors, writers and designers as well as other figures from the forefront of the revolution are invited to consider what it is about stationery that is inspiring such devotion and passion around the world.

Many creatives are returning to an analogue, offline approach because of the unique and charismatic texture that it gives their work; others appreciate the chance it provides to keep and compare preparatory drafts. While nostalgia has a part to play, what we are witnessing is a change in the nature of stationery, not too dissimilar to what has happened to vinyl in recent decades. From a ubiquitous, all-but-invisible necessity, it has become the purist's choice — digital methods may reproduce the effects, but they often lack the soul.

In addition, more and more specialist stationery stores are opening around the world, some of them focused on stationery in general, others on specific products or lines. In *Stationery Fever* we talk to shops from New York to Berlin to Tokyo about their philosophy, their brand and their biggest sellers. Alongside this, we showcase a number of leading contemporary stationery designers, highlighting the most dynamic and beautiful new products on the market.

Of course, the world of stationery is infinitely vast and varied. Here we try to provide an overview of the history of individual stationery items, showing how even the humblest of desktop accoutrements represents the tip of an iceberg of technological progress. Along the way, we find out exactly how they get the lead into pencils, what the eraser has to do with Aztec rituals, and about what John Steinbeck wrote his novels with. The most beautiful and iconic stationery items are considered in depth, alongside more easily overlooked objects that nonetheless had a significant impact, such as the Post-it or drawing pin. And we take a Proustian whiff of PVC glue as we revisit some old classroom classics.

So whether you are a confirmed fanatic or curious beginner, a writer, artist or collector, *Stationery Fever* is an insightful guide to the ever-changing, always fascinating universe of stationery.

CHAPTER Nº 1

PENCIL

———

How the pencil
got its lead

The pencil is a microcosm. The rise and fall of empires, industrialization and mass production, the spread of global capitalism, even the civil rights movement — the stories of all these and more epoch-making developments are contained in miniature in the history of the humble pencil. It is also a miracle of design, the work of thousands upon thousands of inventors, engineers and artists, compressed into a point only a few millimetres wide.

The pencil is a landmark in technical sophistication, its simplicity and universality a testament to the complex processes that led to its creation. Today, it stands for creative spontaneity and freedom, for inspiration and the rough draft. But the history of many disciplines — engineering, architecture, literature — is indivisible from the history of the pencil. And yet, like so much that is familiar, we only notice a pencil when we need one but don't have one to hand. This is why, in order to grasp the truly wondrous nature of the common pencil, not to mention its discreetly instrumental role in world history, we need to see it with fresh eyes.

The name 'pencil' is derived from the word used in Roman times to denote a fine-pointed brush, itself derived from the word *penis*, or tail, its fine tip being made of bristles from animal tails. The word 'pen' shares this origin (as does penicillin, incidentally). Alongside the *penicillum*, the Romans seem to have used metallic lead to make marks on papyrus, but it wasn't until many centuries later that this concept was formalized into something resembling the modern pencil.

By the European Middle Ages, wax tablets were in common use, their chief virtue the fact they could easily be wiped clean and reused — the modern tablet is named for it. Medieval tablets were inscribed with a sort of pointed stylus, and as early as the Twelfth Century a German monk called Theophilus described a variant, a stylus holding a lead/tin alloy used to sketch designs on a wooden board (it is thanks to these early incarnations that we still talk about 'lead' pencils, even though this noxious metal has hardly featured since the days of Theophilus).

We could take this description as evidence that for at least a thousand years humanity has been thinking hard about how to make a dependable, reusable writing implement that could produce uniform lines on an appropriate surface. In fact, if we take charcoal sketches on cave walls to be indicative of the same desire, then there is an argument that the pencil's ancestors emerged at the same time as ours did.

We can, however, be much more precise in dating the first appearance of an unmistakably modern pencil: 1565. This is the year that the Swiss polymath Conrad Gessner published his treatise on fossils *De omni rerum fossilium*, which contains the first known illustration of a pencil. The device he reproduces is in fact somewhat closer to a lead-holder than a pencil in the contemporary sense.

An iron stylus from the European Middle Ages

It comprises a cylinder of 'a sort of lead' (extremely thick by today's standards), inserted into a wooden handle which somehow regulated how much of the lead stuck out at any given moment. 'The stylus shown,' Gessner wrote, 'is made for writing, from a sort of lead which I have heard called English antimony.' This 'English antimony' was the great discovery that gave rise to the birth of the pencil. Although it was referred to by many names during the early stages of the pencil's evolution, the name that was finally hit on was 'graphite', from the Greek verb meaning 'to write'.

It seems that, like the eponymous sausage, graphite originally came from the British county of Cumberland. A pleasing version of the story asserts that an oak tree near the town of Borrowdale was torn down by a storm some time during the reign of Queen Elizabeth I, and among its roots were found various chunks of a black, lead-like mineral that proved useful for marking sheep.

With time, this mysterious substance came to the hands of contemporary creatives, and by 1599 the Italian Ferranti Imperanti was enumerating qualities of the 'grafio piombino' that remain true today: 'it is more convenient for drawing than pen and ink, because the marks made with it appear not only on a white ground, but... also on black; because they can be rubbed out at pleasure; and because one can retrace them with a pen...'

Over the following century, graphite became a valuable commodity. The mine at Borrowdale was protected by royal decree, and the English monopoly on its extraction and sale jealously maintained. Inevitably, however, this monopoly was threatened and eventually broken, thanks to both the exhausting of the Borrowdale mine, and to geopolitical upheavals that obliged countries that had previously depended on English pencils to find ways of substituting them (although there has never since been discovered a significant deposit of such pure and solid graphite).

A cigar is never just a cigar, and a pencil is never just a pencil, no matter how humdrum or domestic it may seem. The great pencil historian Henry Petroski reminds us just how much goes into making one: 'The lead in a single American-made pencil in the late Twentieth Century... might be a proprietary mixture of two kinds of graphite, from Sri Lanka and Mexico, clay from Mississippi, gums from the Orient [sic], and water from Pennsylvania. The wooden case would most likely be made of incense cedar from California, the ferrule possibly of brass or aluminum from the American West, and the eraser perhaps of a mixture of South American rubber and Italian pumice stone.'

A lump of graphite as it looks when it comes out of the ground

HOW PENCILS
ARE MADE

———

One tradition states that it was a joiner in Keswick, a town not far from Borrowdale, who first thought to enclose thin sticks of graphite in wooden casing. But by 1662 a certain Friedrich Staedtler of the city of Nuremberg was registered as a specialized Bleistiftmacher or 'pencil maker' (in fact, it was Staedtler's experimentation with artificial graphite techniques that would pave the way for Conté innovations a century later).

The earliest pencil-making technique was the obvious one, and one that was to remain predominant for several centuries. In short, it involved cutting a strip of wood to a rectangular shape of an appropriate size, and then using a saw to cut a lengthwise groove into it. Graphite was then glued into the groove (there were different ways of doing this) and finally what was to be the fourth face of the rectangle glued on top of it. The pencil was then shaped into, usually, a cylinder or octagon. This is why early pencils had square leads.

Although Conté's process for making graphite changed some details of the pencil production process, variations on the technique established at the outset remained the norm in the centuries preceding the full mechanization of the process. The writer Henry David Thoreau, for example, in his lesser-known role as a pioneer of the American pencil industry, used a method that involved heating a mixture of graphite, glue, wax and spermaceti (a sticky substance found in the heads of sperm whales), and then brushing it into the groove of the wooden case that would later form the basis of the pencil (Thoreau produced a special order of a thousand pencils to finance the publication of his first book).

The big innovation came with the moulding machines used by Dixon in the late 1800s. These worked on a sort of sandwich principle: a cedar wood slat slightly longer than one, the width of six, and the thickness of half a pencil was scored with six lengthwise grooves, each one half the width of a lead. Leads were then placed in each of the grooves, and an identical cedar slat glued on top. This sandwich could then be prepared as required, to create either round or hexagonal pencils. Modern pencils are made in much the same way. The lead is prepared from a mix of graphite and clay powder, with the amount of clay content defining the hardness of the pencil (less clay, softer pencil). This mix is shaped and tempered in a kiln, with the final product being dipped in oil or wax in order to enhance the smoothness of the writing. A key difference is that, where Dixon used cedar, today different types of wood are used, after the American pencil industry denuded the continent of the cedars that were considered to provide the optimum wood for pencil making. Another is that many pencils today sport an eraser at their tip, composed of a metal ferrule holding a rubber plug.

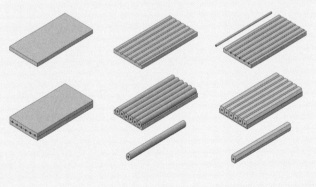

Steps in the pencil making process

An engraving by Nicholas Delauney of pencil innovator Nicholas Jacques Conté (1755–1805)

Of course, it took the world pencil industry a long time to achieve this degree of complexity and diversity, but the first step came on the 1st February 1793, when France declared war on Great Britain, at a stroke losing access to her high quality Borrowdale pencils. Just as the American Civil War later provided a fillip to the domestic pencil industries, and for much the same reasons, it was this event that led the French Minister of War to realize the importance of the pencil, and he commissioned the inventor Nicolas-Jacques Conté to come up with a substitute.

The process Conté hit on involved mixing a finely powdered graphite with clay and water, and then setting it in rectangular moulds. Conté's pencils put the French industry at the forefront of the world scene, displacing the German, based principally in Nuremberg, which had until this point led the way in finding an alternative to Borrowdale graphite. Indeed, many of today's leading pencil manufacturers are still named for the Eighteenth Century German craftsman families that established them — Staedtler and Faber-Castell are still based in the city.

A key factor that enabled competitors to wrest the initiative from the British was the increasing access to other sources of graphite, albeit of inferior quality, that global trade generated. But it was in the New World that pencil technology was truly to come into its own. While an early method used in America to make writing implements involved 'a goose quill, a bullet, a turnip and a ladle', by the mid-1800s the American pencil industry was in furious evolution. This evolution came to mirror, in the second half of the century, the increasing prominence of the machine in American industry.

As has so often been the case, it was an immigrant to the US who was to provide the first significant boost to the industry, namely, the grandson of the founder of Faber pencils. Eberhard moved to the States in 1849, opening the first American pencil factory in Manhattan in 1861, where he put in place one of the earliest mechanized pencil production lines.

Faber's main rival was the entrepreneurial inventor Joseph Dixon, whose Crucible Company was by 1872 producing 86,000 pencils a day. Abraham Lincoln used a German-made pencil to write the Gettysburg Address, or so the story goes, but thanks

PENCIL GRADES

| 9B | 8B | 7B | 6B | 5B | 4B | 3B | 2B | B | HB |

| F | H | 2H | 3H | 4H | 5H | 6H | 7H | 8H | 9H |

As well as developing a new process, it was Conté who first used a numerical system to designate the strength of his pencils (one aspect of his innovation was the ability to control and vary the hardness of the lead). The 'H' (for hard) and 'B' (for black) system that is all but universal today seems to have been pioneered by the British Brookman company. The science of it is relatively straightforward: using less clay in the graphite mix makes the pencil core softer, meaning it will deposit more graphite and thus leave a darker mark; this also means that softer pencils need to be sharpened more often. It has been speculated that it may have been the differing needs of draftsmen that gave rise to this somewhat counterintuitive nomenclature (why not 'H' and 'S'?) Most pencil manufacturers will take account of these varying needs in the packaging of their pencil sets. Derwent, for example, sell a Designer set, ranging from 4H to 6B, a Draughtsman set (9H to B), and a Sketching set (H to 9B).

partly to the mechanization pioneered by Faber and Dixon and partly to the prohibitive import duties imposed on foreign pencils, during Lincoln's administration America reached a point where it was exporting as many pencils as it was importing.

It is noteworthy that it was during this period that the German pencil makers began to lag behind: it was said at the time that the fully mechanized American pencil factories could turn out 50 pencils in the time it took their European rivals to produce just one. It is true that the Germans came increasingly to concentrate on the higher end of the market, but Petroski speculates that their eventual eclipsing was due to the fact that, having achieved a certain degree of technological advancement, 'pencil barons' like Faber began to concentrate on the wellbeing and loyalty of their respective workforces.

The pencil industry has always been closely involved in questions of labour — in fact, the original Nuremberg pencil makers were at the forefront of the dismantling of the old, oppressive guild system and thus played a small but significant part in bringing Europe into the age of industrialization and capitalism. Hundreds of years later, pencil makers were still on the front line of changes in the labour market, when in 1964 Martin Luther King organized a boycott of the pencil company Scripto, which had since the 1920s employed black women almost exclusively, reasoning that they were the workers whom they could pay the least. The protest blossomed and became part of the broader civil rights movement, until it was called off after the company agreed to recognize a union.

According to a point of view that is neither uncontroversial nor indefensible, the traditional wood-cased pencil was perfected in the early Twentieth Century.

Some early (c.1950) Eberhard Faber Mongol pencils in their original packaging

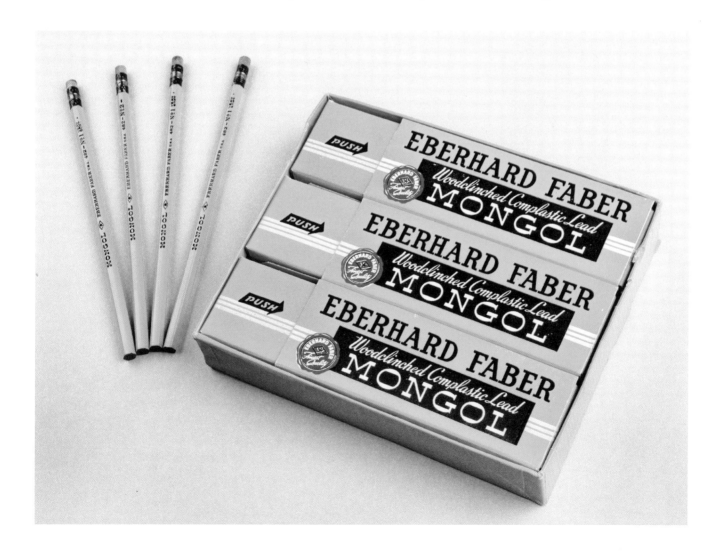

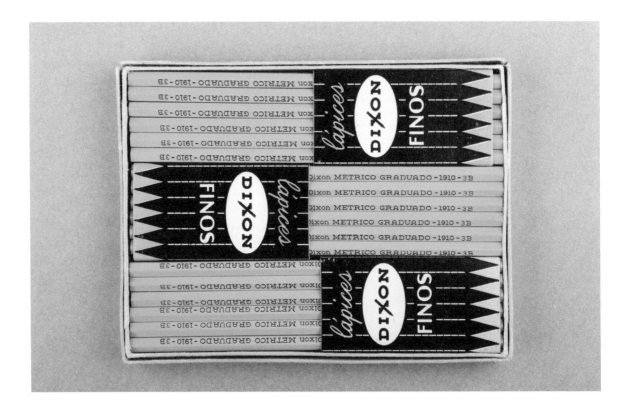

Granted, a certain amount of wheel-reinventing went on thereafter, but following the golden era of the Ticonderoga and the Blackwing, there was really no way that the pencil could be perfected further without its changing into a different kind of artefact altogether.

And this, of course, is exactly what happened. The mechanical pencil (or propelling pencil) is in fact closer in concept to Gessner's pencil than is your average HB: it constitutes a kind of tube with a mechanism inside that regulates how much lead it extends, typically with the click of button. Various versions of the mechanical pencil were developed in the Eighteenth and Nineteenth Centuries — the earliest example we have was found in the wreck of a ship that sank in 1791, while the first spring-loaded mechanical pencil was patented in 1877.
But for different reasons, principally technical, the device didn't take off in a big way until the first decades of the 1900s.

The history of technological development features many cases of two variants on the same breakthrough emerging simultaneously but independently on different parts of the globe. The mechanical pencil is one of these cases. In 1915, Japanese metal worker Tokuji Hayakawa launched his 'Ever-Ready Sharp Pencil', which soon became big in Japan.

The company that grew up around it still bears the name of its first flagship product: Sharp. A year later (to the lasting confusion of pencil historians) the US Eversharp company started to produce mechanical pencils, although these were ratchet- rather than screw-based, as the Japanese incarnation was.

After overcoming certain technical challenges related to the thickness and fragility of the leads, by 1921 twelve million Eversharps had been sold, and within five years' time over a hundred different competitors had set up shop. Part of the reason for this success was that the principle of the Eversharp greatly appealed to pencil-pushers. Remember that at the time almost all office work involved extensive use of pencils. By totting up the wood and lead wasted per traditional pencil, not to mention the cumulative man-hours spent sharpening, salesmen were able to convince bosses of the savings implied by the mechanical pencil.

It was a worldwide hit, and by the '40s there was competition from all quarters. The mechanical pencil never quite succeeded in supplanting its wood-cased cousin, however, despite the convoluted calculations that both sides cooked up to prove their product was, in the end, the more economic. Nevertheless, during the 1970s over

Above: the Eversharp was the first American company to produce mechanical pencils, catapulting the product to worldwide success

Three early leadholders, designed to be refilled with thin rods of lead

Opposite: some rare examples of vintage Dixon pencils produced in Mexico

sixty million mechanical pencils were being produced in the USA each year.

We know what came next. By the 1980s the pencil was already on the wane, although it wasn't until a few years later that the extent of this decline became clear. There has been a meme floating around the internet for a few years, featuring a picture of a cassette with a simple pencil alongside it. Your children, the legend runs, will not understand what these two objects had to do with each other (younger readers may be interested to learn that the tape in a cassette would sometimes come unspooled, and you had to stick a pencil into one of the holes and twizzle it round in order to respool it). For a while it may have seemed like a similar image could simply feature a picture of a pencil with the caption 'Your children won't know what this is.'

And it is true that the pencil will never again be as prominent, widespread or indispensable as it once was. But recent years have shown a growing consciousness of its utility and beauty as an object, and we can be sure that it will never become entirely extinct.

The mysterious symbiosis of pencil and cassette

LEGENDARY PENCILS

Above: a selection of some vintage pencils in their original packaging

The early Twentieth Century was the age of the legendary pencil, almost all of them tributes to the ascendance of the US industry. There was the Czech Koh-I-Noor, named for the world's then largest diamond, a pencil 'with a silken touch as light as a butterfly'; Faber's green-painted Castell, 'the foremost pencil for engineers, technicians and draftsmen', as well as its yellow drawing pencil, the Van Dyke, the elegant Hexagon Gilt, and the Black Monarch; the American Lead Pencil Company's glorious Venus, named for the Venus de Milo, which had a cracked green finish, originally a design flaw in the paint; the Eagle Pencil Company's Turquoise; and Dixon's Eldorado, blue with gold lettering, or their Ticonderoga, patented in 1913, which has acquired mythic status among pencil fanciers worldwide.

SPECIAL PENCILS

_____

Bi-colour pencil. Called at times a postal and at others an editor's pencil, it gives the user rapid access to two different colours of graphite, a valuable feature in a variety of contexts (among them the post office, presumably). The most common model combines blue and red and is typically used for marking or highlighting a page of text; some pencil producers have done a whole range of colour pencils based on this principle.

Universal marker. Manufactured with an oil component in the graphite, these pencils write on glass, china, metal and other polished surfaces. Prior to the invention of the felt pen, these were the only way to write on a surface that was smooth or inhospitable to ink. They are unusual among pencils in that they feature a lid.

Stenographer's pencil. A stenographer is the person in court who makes a shorthand verbatim transcript of all that is said; nowadays they use specialized stenography machines, but previously they relied on one of these pencils. The stenographer could not afford to miss even a few seconds, so it was important for the pencils they used to be entirely reliable: the lead is thus break-proof, and both ends sharpened, just in case. The round shape is designed to be easy on the fingers after a long day's frenzied scribbling.

Copying pencil. First introduced in the 1870s, the copying or indelible pencil's graphite contains a permanent, water-soluble dye. After a sheet was written with it, a further sheet of moist tissue paper was laid atop, and then pressed down with a mechanical press, thus picking up a mirror image of what was written in the original. As du-plicating methods advanced, these pencils came to be used more like proto-ball-point pens. They are extremely injurious to the health, it turns out.

Non-reproducing pencil. These pencils use 'non-photo blue' graphite to make a mark that does not show up in photographic or lithographic reproduction processes. It was traditionally used by editors when correcting texts and, while its necessity has largely been obviated by digital technology, the blue (or red) pencil remains a common metaphor for the editing process. It also gave its name to a legal principle.

Slate pencil. A thin rod of slate, slate pencils are used to write on slate (a slate tablet was, generations ago, how children would take notes in class). Less common nowadays in Europe and the US, they remain a piece of popular classroom equipment in India. Far and away the largest number of references to slate pencils on the internet come from people who are concerned about the quantities in which they eat them: it seems that an urge to gnaw on slate pencils reflects a calcium or other mineral deficiency in your body.

Coloured pencils. Coloured pencils feature a wax- or oil-based core that contains different pigments. Although wax-based materials had been used by artists for centuries, it was only at the beginning of the Twentieth Century that coloured pencils were first manufactured — Faber-Castell put out an artist-grade range in 1908, followed by Caran d'Ache (which remains a benchmark in artists' supplies) in 1924. A key characteristic of artist-grade coloured pencils is their 'lightfastness', or how well they resist the UV rays in sunlight. They generally come in sets, with a set of 72 colours being a fairly standard range. Coloured pencils for students will, for obvious reasons, generally be of a lower quality than artist-grade, and come in a much more limited range. Then there are watercolour pencils — after the drawing has been made, a wet paintbrush can be applied to create a watercolour effect — and pastel pencils — similar to hard pastels, except in that they may be sharpened to a point.

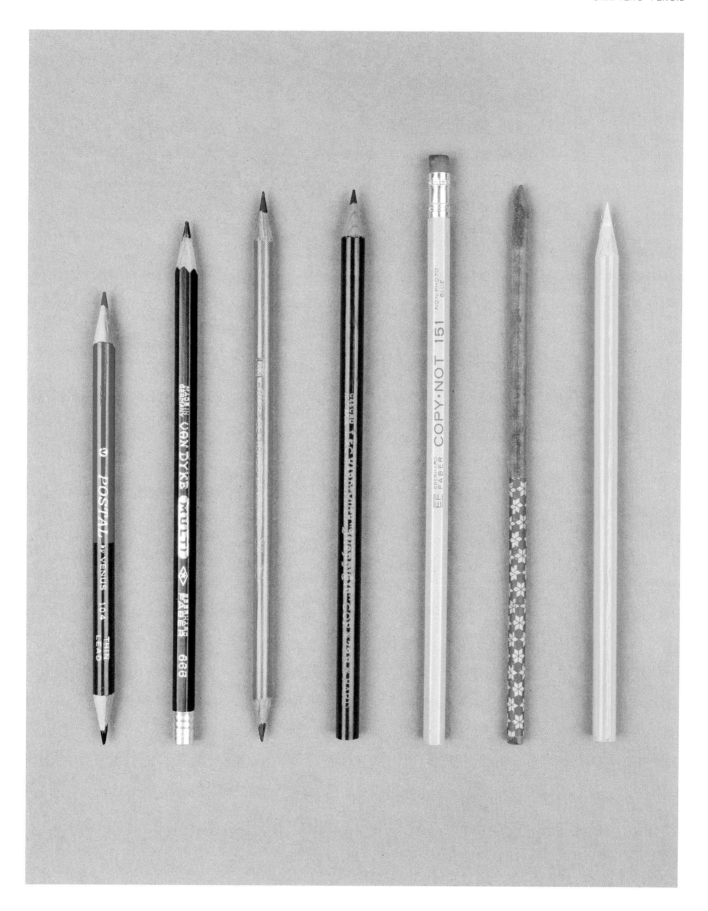

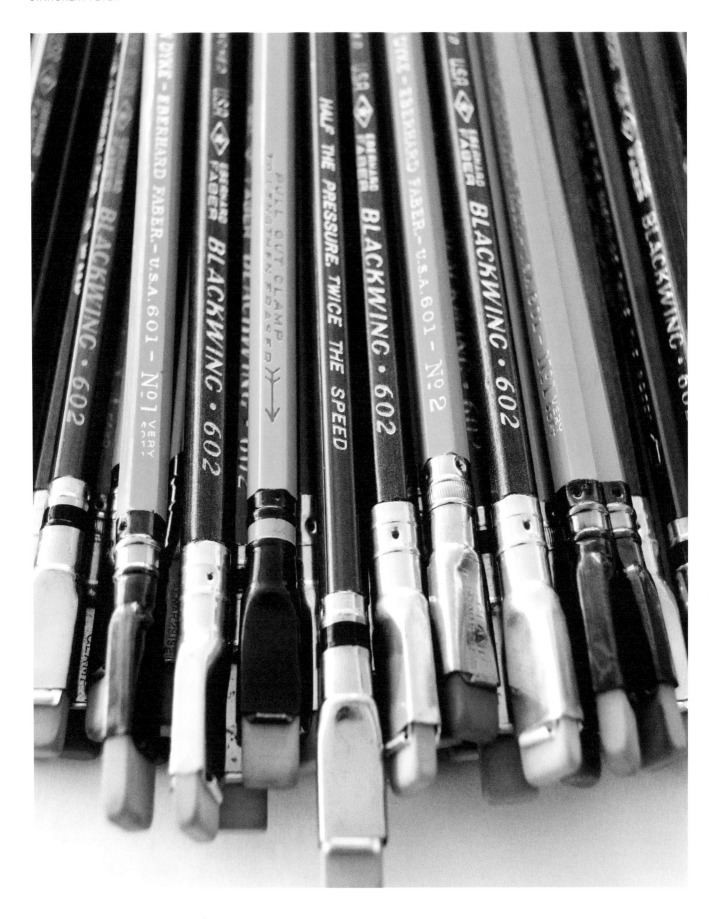

BLACKWING 602

'I have found a new kind of pencil — the best I have ever had... They are called Blackwings and they really glide across the paper...' So wrote John Steinbeck, elsewhere gushing that the pencil 'floated over the paper just wonderfully'. He was talking about the Blackwing 602, the most gorgeous pencil the world has ever seen, and an apogee in the history of industrial design. Steinbeck was far from its only fan: Truman Capote, Chuck Jones, Stephen Sondheim and Eugene O'Neill all swore by them, and the pencil even has a sensual cameo in Vladimir Nabokov's final novel.

Launched in 1934 by Eberhard Faber, this sleek, hexagonal pencil was emblazoned with the legend 'half the pressure, twice the speed', a claim it was able to make thanks to the unique mixture of wax, graphite and clay used in its leads. But what makes the Blackwing most recognizable is the ferrule attached to its tip, which holds in place an eraser. Now, eraser-tips were originally thought up as a gimmick, and remain somewhat pointless — if they don't just snap off, they soon become dirty or wear down to nothing, ruining the look of the pencil. The Blackwing, by contrast, features a 'clamp' mechanism which enables the user to extend and then replace the eraser it contains. The shape of this ferrule also means that the pencil doesn't roll around when set down.

The history and permutations of the Blackwing have been amply documented by world expert Sean Malone on his *Blackwing Pages* blog, where you can find out, for example, that there are at least four variants on the ferrule (the earlier ones being painted the same colour as the body of the pencil, and the later ones gold), or that the earliest Blackwings were painted a colour called 'black steel', later changed for a graphite grey.

For much of the Twentieth Century the Blackwing was a favourite of artists and writers, and people who were prepared to pay for quality. But, big fish in a rather small pond, the pencil was unable to survive the onslaught of the post-industrial era. Eberhard Faber was sold to Faber-Castell in 1988, and then in 1994 bought up by Sanford, which has since become part of the vast Newell Rubbermaid conglomerate. When the machine to make the eraser stopped working in '98, they didn't bother to fix it, meaning that production on the Blackwing simply stopped, another victim of the Office Depot-ing of the stationery world.

Stockpiled by enthusiasts (Sondheim among them) and eulogized in *The New Yorker*, the Blackwing has since undergone apotheosis: unsharpened original 602s routinely fetch up to $50 on eBay. In recent years, however, a company called California Cedar Products bought the rights to the Blackwing trademark, and has begun selling 'Palomino Blackwing' pencils, which are to the untrained eye all but undistinguishable from the original models. Some diehard old-school Blackwing fans are, predictably, unhappy about this, with Sean Malone himself branding the so-called revival 'cultural vandalism'. As to whether the new model is comparable to the old in terms of quality, only a rapidly diminishing number of people are in any position to comment, although the consensus seems to be that the new Blackwing can indeed hold its own. But, beyond questions of authenticity, this new incarnation is indicative of a growing interest in pencils, paper and stationery generally, and is worth celebrating as such.

An assortment of original Blackwing 602s from the collection of Sean Malone

CW PENCIL ENTERPRISE

SHOP, PENCILS	
New York	U.S.A.

The CW Pencil Enterprise was founded in 2014 by 'pencil lady' Caroline Weaver. Its New York store is a pencil fanatic's Aladdin's cave, with every pencil you've ever loved or hankered after (the original Blackwing, for example) pristinely arrayed along the walls; they also customize pencils using a 1960s Kingsley Hot Foil press! Few places in the world constitute such an unequivocal affirmation of the beauty and relevance of the pencil.

"I want to understand how a pencil feels to write with, or what it sounds like to write on different types of paper.

My shop is dedicated to celebrating traditional wood-cased pencils. I spent years collecting and learning about pencils, and realized that there was no one place where all sorts of pencils from all over the world exist together. We sell contemporary pencils, rare antique pencils and specialty pencils, as well as all the things that go with them. We don't have any one type of customer and I really like it that way. We meet a lot of journalists, architects, writers, pencil enthusiasts, school kids, artists — you name it! The one thing about pencil shop patrons is that only nice people shop at specialty pencil shops and I am certainly grateful for that. I get to tell stories and listen to stories all day.

The test station at CW Pencil allows you to find the grade best suited to your needs

An exquisite selection of pencil sharpeners

The big thing for CW Pencil Enterprise is that we know exactly where everything comes from, how it's made and all of the stories related to every pencil. Of course we don't know everything, but it really makes a difference when there's an interesting story to tell. I search for things that are a bit unknown, or things that are interesting, hard-to-find or quite simply classic. Japanese pencils and lesser known European brands are always big sellers because they are often quite difficult to find in the US. We also sell a lot of original Eberhard Faber Blackwing 602s because of their history and rarity. The products that I sell often tell stories of family feuds, manufacturing innovation and patriotism. There is no such thing as a new pencil company, and most of the brands that exist now have been around for at least 80 or 100 years and are family-run. Especially in the US there's a rich history of pencil manufacture in the late 1800s and early 1900s.

We could be categorized as a stationery store but, because we do something very specific, the term stationery has a different meaning and we have to be very careful about the non-pencil things we carry. Everything has to be special, useful and relevant. If we sell paper it has to work well as paper and not be something you can find just anywhere. If we sell greeting cards they have to be made by someone local who we have a relationship with. If we do a collaboration, it has to be with a person or a brand who we really believe in. At the end of the day, everything we sell has to be utilitarian, at least to an extent.

We do have a digital presence, but it is really a small fraction of what we're trying to do. Most customers find us online and then make a point of visiting in person because the shop is such an experience. We sell tactile things, and it's so much nicer to come to the shop, try them out and talk to us about it. That said, even if we can't meet them in person, we try our best to give everyone a memorable experience. I really believe that as technology takes up more space in our lives, things like stationery and handwriting are becoming more important. It may be more of a novelty than a necessity these days, but it always makes my day to see someone re-discover how pleasurable and engaging it is to write with something physical. It's important for cognitive learning and it's important for the purposes of pleasure and nostalgia. I don't think stationery will ever be totally irrelevant.

I personally collect pencils, though I do also use them all (at least once!). I have a really hard time choosing a favorite, but I really love test-scoring pencils. IBM developed them

Each pencil type is displayed in a glass container

A display of the different steps in the pencil making process

Opposite: a home desk mock-up inside the shop

in the 1930s when they came out with the first test scoring machine. The problem with normal natural graphite #2 pencils was that the electrons weren't small enough for the machine to read. To solve the problem, they started making artificial graphite by compressing carbon in a furnace. The result is a really creamy, dark, uniquely shiny mark. There are two US brands that still make a version of this, but we also stock the original IBM ones in various vintages.

My most precious pencils are the ones I collect while travelling or that people give me. Anything with a memory attached to it always has a special place in my collection. And I do have a really hard time not keeping one of everything for myself, but I've started to learn that I appreciate the things I have more if I own fewer of them. No matter how rare a pencil is, I always eventually sharpen it. What makes stationery things and writing instruments so wonderful is knowing what it's like to use them. When we sell out of something before I can get my hands on one I'm always a tiny bit sad, but also happy that so many other people will get to know what it's like to use it."

GIULIO IACCHETTI

PRODUCT DESIGNER

Milan	Italy

Iacchetti is the mastermind behind the Internoitaliano production system, which brings together a network of Italian workshops and manufacturing companies. Their exquisitely simple range embodies the essence of Italian design and material culture. The Neri pen is a masterpiece of contemporary stationery.

"I always thought we would sooner or later have moved the Internoitaliano collection into stationery objects. The opportunity came in the summer of 2015, after a meeting with some friends from Parafernalia, a renowned Italian company that makes designer pens, and where I happened to have worked in the past. I showed them a picture of a pen made from an aluminium rod, they liked it, and so in September I found myself with the first prototypes of the Neri pen and pencil. I knew at once that the project had achieved a goal: the pen was well balanced, the side screw prevented rolling and the refill worked perfectly, allowing for a smooth flow of ink from the tip: I still use those prototypes!

These writing instruments are good examples of a design mode which I call 'new simplicity'. I believe that everyday objects such as pens and pencils should shed all superfluous complexity (such as sophisticated opening and closing mechanisms) in order to recapture simple gestures, such as

a locking screw to close or roll back the refill. I also like mono-materiality and the reduction to the minimum of the work needed to obtain the object that is being created: I believe that all these values are discernible in the Neri project.

You might say that I am the ideal target user of Neri pens. I collect contemporary design pens, but I am always dissatisfied with what I have, and am thus always on the lookout for new things that stimulate my curiosity and satisfy my desire to possess things from which to learn more, and absorb the new lessons that intelligent objects are able to teach us...

Surely every stationery project starts with a writing object: pencils, pens and mechanical pencils are essential elements. The exciting thing is that the desk-object project can be infinitely extended, and made to bring together a wide variety of elements to create a personalisable micro-landscape. Right now we are planning a big family of corollary Neri objects: a desk clock, small containers, scissors, letter openers. These are classic elements, but we are also thinking about other things, including a little bell, an ashtray and more. The goal is to conceive a desktop that is able to represent the personality of the person who uses it. I do look

The sleek, minimal design of the
aluminium propelling pencil is enhanced
by a vintage touch lent by the screw

at the collections of competitors, but mostly for inspiration
I let myself be guided by my instincts. I look for objects that
haven't been over-worked by designers, but that still play
an important role in the home. Using design to bring these
objects into line with contemporary tastes is one of the keys
to the success of Internoitaliano.

Among the stationery brands that I love are Lamy and the
Tombow design collection, which in the '90s was an incredibly
cool stationery alternative, a set of pens and mechanical
pencils with a notable visual impact, each one very different,
but together constituting a family held together by a special
feeling. Naturally, I own all of them, but it would be a
beautiful goal to one day work for the company. Finally, I
couldn't fail to mention Moleskine, for whom I designed the
writing, travelling and reading collection."

THE ERASABLE PODCAST

PENCIL COMMUNITY	
ONLINE	U.S.A.

Hosted by Johnny Gamber, Tim Wasem and Andy Welfle, The Erasable Podcast is aired every other week. After 45 episodes covering everything from 'literature to carpentry, accounting to space travel', it has become a focus for the pencil community worldwide.

How did you come up with the concept for the show? Did it emerge fully formed or has it evolved with time?

ANDY: The show started after a few weeks of Tim and me having a conversation on Twitter. I was a guest on *The Pen Addict* and at some point after, Tim asked, 'have you ever thought about doing a pencil podcast?' In fact, I had, but I knew I couldn't do it on my own. Tim and I both knew we had to get Johnny on board — he was a heavyweight (the original pencil blogger) and a super friendly guy. As for the show's format, we always knew we wanted to keep it super casual and mostly just be three voices talking about pencils. From the moment we first chatted, we had a great chemistry that showed us that would could pull off a bi-weekly podcast about pencils. We've evolved into a somewhat more structured program, with a couple segments and a transition from follow-up to our main topic, and we've acquired better audio equipment and editing, but generally, it's the same show as it was 45 episodes ago.

Presenters Johnny and Andy with Tim on the phone

Johnny alongside the sculpture of a typewriter eraser
by Claes Oldernburg and Coosje van Bruggen

Could you summarize your philosophy?

TEAM: We're celebrating and sharing our love of analogue
writing tools like wooden pencils, and pencil accessories.

Just what is it about pencils?

TEAM: Good question! There are plenty of reasons, both
practical and philosophical. Andy's written about it a few
times, but most notably, using a pencil is maybe the purest
form of writing without getting your fingers dirty. There's
essentially no difference between writing with your pencil
and drawing on a cave wall with a charred stick. Sure, the
formula has been refined, and the stick has been encased in
wood. But in practice, it's the same — just rub some carbon off
onto a flat surface. It's built into your psyche; your ancestors
have been doing it for tens of thousands of years. In addition,
the best wooden pencil you can buy isn't more than three or
four dollars. Graphite is fade-proof and waterproof. Pencil
truly is forever. And they're so interesting to look at!

**There is surely no denying that pencils, and stationery in
general, are seeing a new surge of interest around the world.
Why do you think this is? Is it sustainable, or just a trend?**

TEAM: We read something recently about millennials and
how they're becoming more and more interested in analogue
experiences. The article was mostly about vinyl and why
they'd buy a turntable rather than just download something
from Apple Music or Spotify, but the same holds true for
stationery. Sure, Microsoft Word may be more efficient, but
writing longhand with a pencil in a notebook gives you a
tactile experience and slows you down, forcing you to think
about the words coming out of your brain. We've been accused
of being hipsters, but I think we and those in our community
have a genuine, unironic love for precisely these reasons.

**Much is made of the incompatibility of digital and analogue
techniques — can the two approaches to creativity be reconciled?**

ANDY: Absolutely it can. I work at a very large tech company
in Silicon Valley, and I see notebooks and pens all around
me, even among software engineers who work deep in code
all day. I think that there's an element of analogue creation
that just can't be met digitally right now, even though
companies like Apple are trying hard with their iPad Pro
and Apple Pencil.
JOHNNY: Hemingway wrote his fiction in longhand and

The Erasable community banner is styled on the original Blackwing 602 packaging

later typed up words up or had them typed up. He'd probably use a laptop instead of a typewriter before sending off his drafts today. The two approaches are two sides of the same activity. Analogue is more personal and intimate, and digital approaches enable us to take our work to our community.

The Palomino Blackwing pencil has caused a lot of controversy. What is your take on it?

ANDY: I worked at CalCedar (the parent company of the Palomino brand), so I may not be the best person to talk about it. I think, though, that it can be a rough transition to resurrect a brand (in this case, Eberhard-Faber's Blackwing to Palomino's Blackwing) that many people have known and loved for decades, to something new that's trying to innovate yet stay true to the original. Palomino had incredible pencils for years before the new Blackwings came out, so they have a deep knowledge of good pencilry to back it up. If anyone can create new products while honouring the heritage of the original, it's them.

Which pencil, which eraser, and which pencil sharpener would you take with you into exile?

ANDY: That's a hard one, especially since a pencil will eventually disappear as you use it! I think, though, that I'd take a pack of Palomino Golden Bears with me, along with a KUM Masterpiece sharpener (to get that super long point) and perhaps a Koh-i-noor 'Magic' eraser, if only because it's so darn pretty.
JOHNNY: I would take a box of naturally-finished pencils (General's Cedar Pointe HB, Ticonderoga Renew, or Palmino Forest Choice) and a very sharp knife. I don't really use erasers much, to be honest.

R.S.V.P.	
SHOP, STATIONERY	
Berlin	Germany

R.S.V.P. was founded in 2001 in Berlin's hip Mitte neighbour-hood. In 2014, R.S.V.P. opened a second shop across the street from the first, with interior design by architect Manolis Iliakis. Selling fine paper and writing materials from around the world, R.S.V.P. has been selected as one of the best stores in Berlin by *Time Out*, Louis Vuitton and *Elle*, among many others. Meike Wander has run the store and online shop since 2004.

"R.S.V.P. opened 15 years ago. The idea behind the store was to offer a selection of well-designed, durable everyday products, not luxury, but good quality and good design. The aim was to offer an alternative to the cheap plastic pens and PhotoPrint notebooks made of cheap white paper that flooded every household, and to banish this ugliness from everyday life. Back then, that was not so easy. In the stationery segment there were either poorly designed cheap, disposable products, or prestige, luxury goods. It was a new idea that a nice pen could reflect good taste rather than just wealth.

I think the typical customer of R.S.V.P. shares these ideas, and are less interested in status symbols than in good design and interesting materials. For us, the webshop is important because it attracts customers from all over the world and here they can get a first impression: it is an important business card. But online shopping lacks the materiality that is so important when it comes to paper and to good design. I for one can only get excited if I have found a beautiful combination of products on the shelf of a shop, if I can feel the surface of some paper, the body of a pen, the coolness of the metal, the warmth of wood.

My personal favourite stationery item is the Caran d'Ache 849 pen. It has been available at R.S.V.P. from the very beginning, and there was not a day when I felt it was out of fashion or didn't fit. For me this pen is a prime example of good design and excellent quality. It will always be beautiful, and always work. But it remains still a basic, simple commodity. It doesn't show off, it simply does its duty.

There are a few things that I own that have been in my drawer for many years, and now and then something is added, although fortunately this doesn't happen so often. These are usually the most trivial objects: old school books from Greece, or from East Germany, my grandmother's Koh-I-Noor pencils, a packet of paper clips…

Currently there is quite a lot of hype around stationery. One result of this is that at the moment perhaps our biggest challenge is defining what we sell. The market for stationery has become so large, and the line is becoming increasingly blurred between stationery and what is really a design object/decoration. I would define 'stationery' as things that have utility value around the office or on the desk. An object that blurs the line is, for example, the paperweight — although it has a use value on the desk, it is usually outweighed by its decorative character. Dealing with this limit is a daily balancing act.

One reason for this hype is the process of aestheticization of everyday life that has long been observed by sociologists. Today, the most mundane everyday objects have distinguishing features. And of course this complete design of the self includes the everyday objects you can find in stationery shops. The office and the kitchen are workplaces of everyday life, for which there are a multitude of small but vital commodities. If they don't work well it annoys you for

the whole day, and if they are ugly, you will be irritated all day by their presence.

If they are well-designed and functional, by contrast, as well as durable and pleasing to the eye, then it's fun to use them. It makes a huge difference, for example, if a stapler can only be used forcefully and makes a clunky sound, or whether it is a perfectly fitting clamp that makes a beautiful click as it slides effortlessly into the paper. One can even enjoy writing a shopping list, with a good pen that slides over the smooth paper instead of scratching it. And this is where the obsession begins. Saving yourself from ugliness is not only a relief, it's a pleasure, and this awakens in us this lustful admiration for the object."

Opposite, top: display of the twin shop's selection of wrapping paper

What characterizes the selection of products stocked by R.S.V.P. is a minimal and timeless aesthetic

CHAPTER Nº 2

SHARPENER

The fine art of
getting to the point

Sharpening a pencil is, above all, an aesthetic experience. And like all true aesthetic experiences, sharpening a pencil brings into play several of the senses, together and singly and in different combinations throughout the course of the process. The first sense it activates is, naturally, the visual. A pencil aficionado knows to extract every last drop of sensory pleasure from their interactions with stationery, and will always have an attractive pencil sharpening device occupying a coveted slice of desk space.

Previous spread: Pencil shavings in an acrylic box, product of Nakajima Jukyudo

Below: a selection of pencil and lead sharpeners, showing the great taxonomic rage of designs

A sharpener may be visually attractive for different reasons: thanks to its sleek, cutting edge design, perhaps, or to its status as a sought-after antique. This visual thrill is then heightened by the smooth, satisfactory nature of the action of inserting, twisting and sharpening the pencil, culminating in curlicues of shavings.

The second of the two senses principally engaged by pencil sharpening is the tactile — a beautiful pencil sharpener will be distinguished by how it interacts with the hand, whether it is fixed down or placed in the palm. And, whilst the visual and the tactile are the senses that preside over pencil sharpening, the aural and the olfactory also come into play, because the acoustic pleasure provided by the whirr of a finely-tuned mechanism is undeniable, as is the aroma of freshly cut wood.

But sharpening a pencil is no less fruitful or fascinating a pursuit for a lover of science and design than it is for the epicure, as the sharpener in many ways represents an apogee of engineering. Few devices have embodied so perfectly, so compactly the core goals of technological progress, as we will now discover.

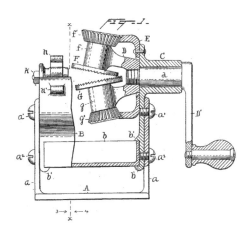

Leonhard Dingworth's *Kleine Anspitzer-Fibel. Von den Anfängen bis 1960. Geschichte, Beschreibungen und Abbildungen von Spitzern und Spitzmaschinen* (2008) is the most breathtakingly comprehensive history of the pencil sharpener yet published. Sadly for those ignorant of the German language, it has yet to be published in English, although its lushly illustrated pages are a delight to all.

Dingsworth provides us with a classificatory system that breaks pencil sharpeners down into two main categories: hand sharpeners and mechanical sharpeners. Hand sharpeners he divides into three sub-categories: simple blades or knives; those that rely on filing or sanding; and manual sharpeners. Mechanical sharpeners he divides among: mechanical sanding tools; sharpeners with star-shaped blades; sharpeners with disk mills; sharpeners with side mills; and miscellaneous others. Dingsworth's system will provide us with a handy guide as we examine the early stages of the history of the pencil sharpener. Given that his purview concludes in 1960, he omits the electrical sharpener, which we will examine in its turn. For now, all we need to do is bear in mind that there are essentially three types of sharpener: hand (or small, or pocket, as they are sometimes known), mechanical, and electric.

For centuries, the only way to bring your pencil to a point was by shaving away the wood casing from one end, until the graphite once again emerged into a sharp tip. But sharpening a pencil using a knife was very far from an intuitive skill. While the cedar wood used in the first pencils mass-produced in the USA lent itself to controlled and accurate cutting, it took much practice to shape the cone correctly and at the same time avoid the fatal cut-too-far that results in the graphite being lopped off and the whole process having to be repeated. In addition, whether you whittled away from or towards the body, it was hard not to soil the fingers, adding further time and effort to the whole process. This advertising copy discovered by Henry Petroski lays out how time-consuming knife sharpening was, and makes clear that the drive to modernize was as ever inspired by a desire for increased efficiency in the workplace: 'Borrowing neighbour's knife, two minutes; sharpening pencil, three minutes; washing hands on company's time, five minutes.'

But the prehistory of the pencil sharpener stretches back further than the early modern office, to Waterloo vet Constant de Thierry des Estivaux, who in 1847 patented his design for a tube fitted with a blade inside a narrowing cone (the prototypical incarnation of Dingsworth's hand sharpener

Above: massed ranks of aluminium and brass pencil sharpeners

Below: the A. B. Dick Planetary Pencil Pointer

with a simple blade). Although other Europeans before him had flirted with the idea, it was Constant de Thierry who produced the device that can truly be said to have kickstarted the development of the modern sharpener. It was thanks to his work that towards the end of the Nineteenth Century a tipping point was reached in the USA, and a flurry of patents applied for within the span of only a few years, each one surpassing its immediate predecessor in one small element.

As we have seen, antique mechanical sharpeners fall into different categories, based on the method they employed to shave away at the pencil tip. One used abrasion, either sandpaper or a file, as in the case of the steampunky Gem Pencil Sharpener, patented by Gould & Cook in 1886 and weighing in at more than 3kg, which featured a rotating sandpaper disk for sharpening the pencil (turning a miniature mangle-crank made both disk and pencil rotate).

It was, unsurprisingly, the big names in the pencil biz who were the ones keenest to get ahead in sharpening, and it was they who began streamlining in earnest. The early mechanical sharpeners are perhaps best represented by the Dixon's Pencil

Sharpener, first released in 1885, a gorgeous affair featuring several cranks and gears, as well as a conical piece into which the pencil was inserted and then rotated against an inwardly-projecting blade.

As with the pencil, the handheld pencil sharpener seems to have been perfected in the earlier part of the Twentieth Century and, gimmicks aside, the small metal sharpener that today's schoolchildren use it not that different to what their grandparents carried in their pencil cases. The mechanical pencil sharpener likewise achieved a degree of perfection fairly early on, and their modern incarnation — whether affixed to the desk or free-standing — has a lot in common with the versions in use in the '20s and '30s.

The basic principle of the mechanical pencil sharpener is as follows: they feature a set of cylindrical cutters, locked in place within the mechanism and set at a diverging angle. A pencil is inserted into the relevant hole and a crank on the outside turned, and the cutters in tandem sharpen the pencil to a point; using 'planetary gears', as they are known in engineering, these sharpeners are often known as 'planetary sharpeners'. Variants on this model may include a spring-driven holder, which pulls the pencil into the sharpener,

Above: the Janus 1 sharpener

Below: a playful novelty sharpener design

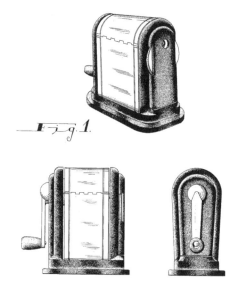

Fig. 1.

Above: design patent 152554. February 1st, 1949, for a mechanical sharpener based on the Ranger Boston 55

Below: UNI ES10 electric pencil sharpener

a repository for the shavings, or a dial to modulate sharpness. As we have seen, the basic idea of the planetary sharpener having been hit on at an early stage in its development, the mechanism itself did not evolve overmuch in the following decades. And in fact the next major step forward for the pencil sharpener did not involve a significant modification of its inner workings, so much as of the means by which it worked.

A report quoted in the Early Office Museum's 'Antique Electric Pencil Sharpener Gallery' describes how a worker on a pencil production line in 1914 operates the electrical sharpening device: 'He thrusts a dull pencil into the electrically driven sharpener. For a brief moment it is held in place, then at exactly the right moment, without hesitation or a false move, the pencil is withdrawn, topped by a perfect point.'

This industrial technology was soon adapted to the domestic market (basically by replacing the crank on a hand-turned mechanical pencil sharpener with a battery or connection to the mains) where it had secured an important position by the 1930s. John Steinbeck, ever the pencil lover's pencil lover, sung its praises: 'I have never had anything that I use more and was more help to me.'

THE GRENADE
by Gunther Schmidt

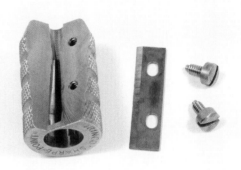

In the beginning, pencils were usually sharpened with the same penknife that was used for the goose quill. Later, resourceful minds invented a wide range of devices intended to make the sharpening process easier, but none was more successful than the tapered pencil sharpener whose invention was credited to the London branch of the French company A. Marion & Co. According to a reliable source, a manual sharpener manufactured using the same process and known as the Grenade came on the market in around 1890, approximately 40 years after Marion's invention. Essential details have been lost — despite its great popularity, we no longer know who came up with the idea for its characteristic shape, who originally produced and sold it. Its baptism, on the other hand, is documented: in March 1901, the 'Warenzeichenblatt' (trademark register) of the Imperial Patent Office records the registration of the trademark Grenade under the number 47683 by Cologne stationery wholesalers Möller & Breitscheid.

The design of the Grenade, rather unusual compared with that of other manual sharpeners, has changed little over the decades. It has retained its cylindrical shape with the four knurled grip zones and tapered point; only the attachment of the blade has been revised. While the blade was originally held in position by two pins and a knurled screw, it is now secured in the knife bed with positive locking and held by only one screw. Variants such as the Sharpe-Point manufactured In England by Brinco were of slightly different design; there was also a version for thicker pencils and one with a wooden grip intended to prevent the user's fingers becoming soiled.

Today's Grenade is made by the traditional manufacturing company Möbius+Ruppert, based in Erlangen, Franconia. As in the old days, it is made of brass, a durable tool that becomes even more attractive with age. The blade, with a hardness between that of a Swiss army knife and a Japanese chef's knife, is replaceable, making the Grenade a lifelong companion. The pencil may disappear with use, but the Grenade that sharpens it will remain — and has done so for well over 100 years.

HOW TO SHARPEN PENCILS

A PRACTICAL and THEORETICAL TREATISE on the ARTISANAL CRAFT of PENCIL SHARPENING

for:
- writers
- artists
- contractors
- flange turners
- anglesmiths
- civil servants

WITH ILLUSTRATIONS SHOWING CURRENT PRACTICE

DAVID REES
"The number one #2 pencil sharpener"

With a Foreword by
JOHN HODGMAN

PROFESSIONAL SHARPENER

| New York | U.S.A. |

Renowned humorist and cultural critic David Rees in July 2010 announced the launch of his Artisanal Pencil Sharpening service, 'perfect for artists, writers, and standardized test takers'. He invites clients to send in their blunt pencil to be sharpened according to the 'age-old art of manual pencil sharpening'. *The New Yorker* called Rees' book on the subject, *How to Sharpen Pencils*, 'the standard to which all future pencil-sharpening textbooks must now aspire'.

What was it that first sparked your interest in the art of pencil sharpening?

I had a job working for the U.S. Census in 2010. All the forms were to be filled out with a #2 HB pencil. So on the first day of staff training we were instructed to sharpen our pencils. I thought it was fun and wondered if there was a way I could get paid to sharpen pencils. It was like a challenge: How would I have to market my services in order to convince people to pay me to do something they usually did for themselves? That's why I decided to call it 'Artisanal' pencil sharpening. The artisanal movement was getting very popular, so I decided to adapt its language and aesthetics for this everyday task of sharpening pencils. In order to call myself an 'artisan' I had to do research on different sharpening techniques, and develop new ways of refining pencil points. I wanted to give my customers an unusual pencil-sharpening experience, something that would make it worth their money. That's why I bag and return the shavings along with the pencil, and why I send along a signed Certificate of Sharpening with every pencil.

Broadly speaking, what is essential to the craft of pencil sharpening?

At its most basic, all you need is an unsharpened pencil and some sort of abrasive or cutting material with which to fashion a usable point. I have a lot of sharpeners, knives, etc. I also have sanding blocks for refining the graphite once it's been exposed by the sharpener/knife blades. I buy vinyl tubing from a hardware store and cut it to fit around the sharpened pencil point — this protects the point in transit. I use clear plastic shatterproof tubes to ship the pencils. I wear a black apron to keep my shirts clean, because it can get pretty messy.

What makes for a good sharpener (person not tool)?

Patience and attention to detail. You have to be willing to let go, too: Because your perfect pencil point is going to disappear with use.

What makes for a good sharpener (tool not person)?

Sharp blades and heavy-duty construction. You want to be able to remove the blades for re-sharpening or replacing. If you're using a pocket sharpener (i.e. the kind you twist the pencil in) make sure the tiny blade is sitting properly in the sharpener's body so that it produces an even conical point on the pencil.

You have detailed your experience with the deluxe 'El Casco' sharpener. Do you have any, perhaps more affordable, recommendations for the armchair sharpener?

There's a good hand-crank sharpener you can order from ClassroomFriendlySupplies.com. It produces a long point. I've seen this model marketed under different names and distributed in different countries, but I have a feeling they're all made in the same factory in China.

If you had to choose one pencil sharpener to take with you to a desert island, which would it be, and why?

My grandfather's pocket knife, for sentimental reasons. Also if I'm on a desert island, it could be used for more than just sharpening pencils.

You write of how you 'jettisoned all emotion and declared myself a psychological eunuch with nothing to live for beyond pencils'. What do you think it is about pencils that makes them induce this response?

There are many kinds of pencil nerds out there: Collectors, draftsmen with specific preferences, etc. Pencils are an inexpensive, elegant tool of communication. They also have a lot of history, since they have been around since the mid-Sixteenth Century. In addition to the overall history of pencils, people often have strong nostalgic associations with specific pencil brands from their youth. They are one of the few tools that just about everybody has used at one point in their life.

Your book is, of course, about more than just sharpening pencils. What?

In addition to being a how-to manual, it's also a memoir about a specific, weird time for me: my wife and I had split up and I wasn't sure what I was doing with my life or my career. It's also an argument for never taking anything for granted. I like the idea that something as simple and familiar as a pencil can reveal itself to be really interesting and beautiful once you start focusing on it in a new way. That's why I put so much strange stuff in the book — I wanted to make pencils feel weird and unfamiliar and magical.

The Tsunago pencil sharpener is the revolutionary creation of bleeding edge Japanese company Nakajima Jukyudo. By way of a simple but effective three-holed design, users are able to recycle their pencil stubs and create their own Frankenstein's pencil. The Tsunago is a unique and canny bit of industrial design which is provoking a lot of interest among pencil fans worldwide.

Nakajima Jukyudo was founded in 1933, and pioneered a resin manufacturing process. 1940 was the year in which it started to shape the resin into pencil sharpeners, and after the war it developed the first plastic mould-injection machine ever built in Japan, setting itself up as a pioneer in plastic injection pencil sharpeners. The company now specializes exclusively in plastic pencil sharpeners, and makes around 80% of the sharpeners sold in Japan, producing over 6 million a year, for every kind of pencil.

Nakajima Jukyudo produces all its parts in-house. The blades are quenched, cooled and tempered in the company kiln, and then go through a five-stage polishing process before being finished at a tolerance of 0.03 to 0.04mm. Junya Nakajima, the third president of the company, always handles this micron-level stage in the process, as it demands faultless artistry.

It is this commitment to precision and quality that has earned Nakajima Jukyudo a worldwide reputation (it is one of MoMA's official goods suppliers). It has recently been gaining attention for its Tsunago line of pencil sharpeners. These three-holed sharpeners function in a relatively straightforward way: rotating a pencil stub in one hole allows users to bore a recess hole into the back end; another hole is used to shape another stub so that it fits in the recess hole, and the two may be joined together. This process can be repeated several times to create a full-sized, absolutely unique, tatterdemalion pencil.

Opposite: a Tsunago pencil sharpener in action. The three settings of the sharperner are shown, and above them the results

Above: animal-shaped pencil sharperners frolic and cavort

Below: their attention to presentation and general aesthetics has earned Nakajima Jukyudo a worldwide following

klammer stäbe

VEB METALLVERARBEITUNG · LEIPZIG

Barock

STEMPELKISSEN

Pelikan SPECIAL 32

Läufer CORALL - 620

W. GERMANY

HARDTMUTH "KOH-I-NOOR" COP × 1561 × E

1000
24/6

Heftklammern verkupfert ®

LACO

● Staples coppered ● Agrafes cuivré ● Grapas encobrado

INKWELL
BERLIN

SHOP, VINTAGE	
Berlin	Germany

Inkwell is a shop, a studio and a venue. Launched in 2015 in Berlin's Neukölln neighbourhood, the philosophy of the shop is based on recuperating beautiful stationery objects from the past, selected for their function as much as their form. Inkwell sells a mixture of classic pieces, mixed with cutting edge contemporary design.

"One of the things that makes Inkwell such a dynamic place is that it is a hybrid — we have the shop and the press, as well as a studio and a venue where we organize events related to stationery and publishing. And Inkwell Press grew out of the shop. Here we use period Mimeograph and Risograph machines to print artworks, books and magazines. We mainly concentrate on obsolete printing techniques; our Stationery Survival Kits feature packaging that we design and print ourselves. Neukölln is a real melting pot of artists and likeminded people, and we have organized a lot of printing workshops with cutting edge creatives.

The Inkwell team has a strong background in industrial design; we're crazy for interesting objects that work in unexpected ways. We find the material we sell in a lot of places. We don't have any stock and what we have on display is what there is. Germany has always been one of the biggest producers of stationery in the world, so we have a lot of

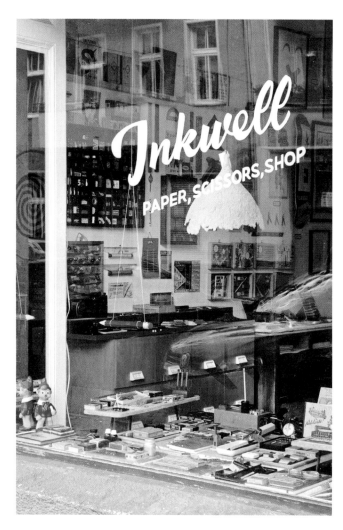

Previous spread: Composition of vintage stationery products at Inkwell Berlin

Above: the beautifully curated shop window at Inkwell Berlin, featuring an interesting mix of vintage and modern designs

Right: a selection of period office equipment

beautiful vintage German stationery, in particular a lot of things from the former East and West Germany. Another thing we can't get enough of is Italian design, above all from around the middle of the last century — we sell a lot of vintage notebooks and nibs. We recently went on a buying trip to Mexico and came back with some really gorgeous pieces. And of course we have things from many other places: Russia, Poland, France, the US.

In addition, we have hosted a presentation of Russian artist Olya Bazilevich's print works; a talk by writer Craig Schuftan on his use of index cards; and the launch of the book *The Wolpertingers* by the poet Conor Jack Creighton and illustrator Harriet Richardson. The stationery line My Own Books was launched out of Inkwell, as was the great *Lazlo Magazine*, and a joint stationery project with the Japanese designer Jiyucho. And the shop features a beautiful paper sculpture of a giant broken pencil by Wenhui Zheng.

We sell a lot of obsolete items that have a nostalgic thrill for people — we sold some slate pencils and a slate writing tablet this morning to a lady who had used them in school — as well as more peculiar or unexpected things that call people's attention — interesting devices, for example, or uncommon artist's supplies. A popular product are leadholders, like the Eversharp, and higher-end vintage pens: this month we sold a Parker 51, a Lamy Safari, and several antique German makes. It was particularly hard to say goodbye to a pair of '70s Pelikan Graphos.

One of our specialities is pencils. We have a lot of vintage pencils in the original packages of 12: Venus, Eagle, Dixon Ticonderoga, Hardtmuth Mephisto, and of course the Eberhard Faber Mongol, the world's most perfect pencil. At Inkwell we are fascinated by how each object has its own story, by the small details. We love to find out how each piece came to be created, about how one invention led to another. Stationery is about centuries of perfection, and each object we

A selection of the vintage Mexican, Italian and East German stationery items on sale at Inkwell Berlin

stock is imbued with history. Approaching stationery with this historical perspective really helps you to appreciate the small details — how a new, more viscous ink made the ball-point pen possible, for example.

It also helps you to see afresh the most everyday items. Maybe it's an obvious example, but the paper clip is a totally unpretentious and utterly ubiquitous object, yet there are few others that embody so perfectly and compactly the essence of the Bauhaus aesthetic of the elegance of function. Or there's the highlighter pen, which today we take for granted, but when it was invented constituted a breakthrough in terms of technology and design, and which has come to impact on the way we read, the way we learn.

Working on a computer is always a metaphor. Whichever action you perform, it is always transformed into, mediated by, pixels, never the real thing. Using stationery helps you to re-establish that contact with the material, with the medium. Imagine doing all your cooking via an app — even if the final product is a physical object, there is no substitute for a direct, hands-on relationship with the thing itself.

That is what we try and do at Inkwell, with the shop, the studio and the press. Without rejecting digital techniques, we try to bring people back into contact with physical, tactile, tangible reality. And they keep coming back."

Screen-printed, 1970s Italian notebooks

PAPIER TIGRE

PRODUCER, SHOP

Paris	France

Formed in 2011 by Paris-based graphic designers, Papier Tigre is a collective that makes a range of lush paper-based products. Their distinctive patterns and styles are featured on notebooks and stationery, clothing and accessories, and furniture and ornaments. The original Paris store was recently complemented by the opening of a Berlin branch, putting Papier Tigre at the forefront of European design.

"We started to work on the first Papier Tigre products in 2011. We were also working in a creative studio at the time, but we were more excited by our own project than our clients' projects, and we wanted to give it a try. It became serious very quickly, and today we are 100% focused on Papier Tigre.

The idea was to use our creativity. At first we were more interested in stationery and how to move this very old-style business, but we have come to work on more decorative and playful items. Creativity is still the core of our business, and it always will be. In fact, we call ourselves a creative brand, not a stationery brand. We get inspiration from everything! We draw on our everyday lives in Paris and Berlin, things like exhibitions, galleries, the cinema, concerts, and so on. We also travel quite often to North America and Japan, and that gives us a lot of new ideas to bring to life!

Above: objects personalized
with Papier Tigre adhesives

Left and below: the hot foil stamping
process used to emboss the gold
Papier Tigre logo, giving their range of
products a unique and stylish touch

Among our most popular products are The Greengrocer (that helps to remind you about the fruits and vegetables you can find according to the seasons) and The Manager (for office organisation). The cardboard A5 notebooks are also big sellers. Our favourite products are those we make and conceive with others; collaborations are very interesting to us. For instance, the Japane ceramic plates collection is very important. We worked with one of the most traditional and oldest factories: it was really rewarding when we received the plates here in Paris. We also worked with Beams in Japan for a special edition of Kendama (a Japanese Bilboquet). The sales support people affected by the recent earthquake in the north of the country — and we feel very honoured to be able to help them with our creativity."

The sumptuous Papier Tigre notebook range, in a characteristic range of tones that combines the bold and the muted

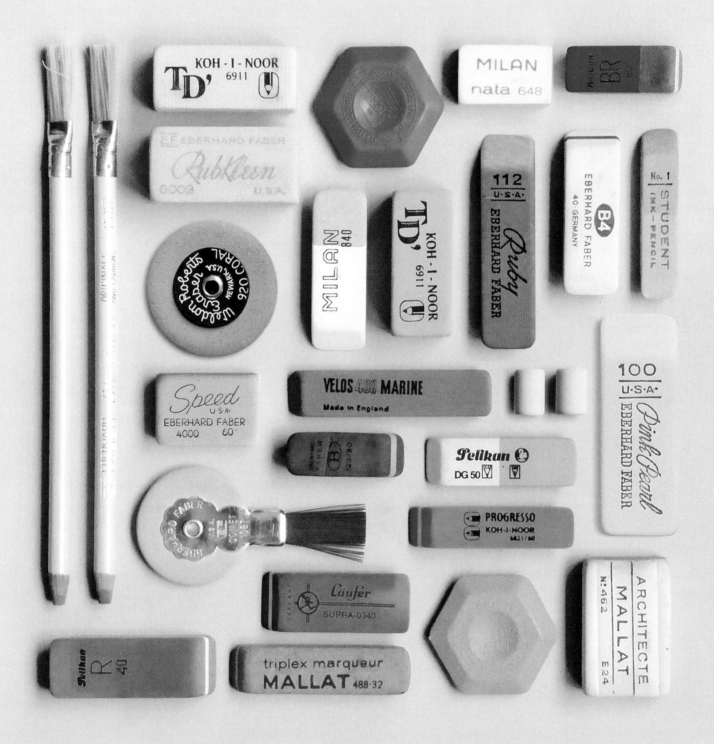

CHAPTER Nº3

ERASER

———

We all deserve
a second chance

The history of the eraser starts with the Olmecs. One of the first significant civilizations in Mesoamerica, the Olmecs pre-dated the Aztecs by about a thousand years and very little of their culture has come down to us. We don't even know what they called themselves: Olmec comes from an Aztec word meaning 'rubber people', a reference to the fact the Olmecs were the first society on the planet to produce rubber, by harvesting milky, sap-like 'natural latex' and mixing it with the juice from morning glory vines.

Previous and current spread: a
panopoly of beautiful erasers,
among them the iconic Pink Pearl

Not that the Olmecs used their rudimentary rubber for
erasing things, given that the pencil wasn't to emerge until
2,000 years later. One thing they did make with it was the
ball for the mysterious, ritual ball game they invented,
the losing teams of which, it seems, were decapitated.
And the Aztecs used rubber to make a sort of flip flop.

The knowledge of rubber technology spread from the Olmecs
across South America. Indeed, the French word for natural
rubber is 'caoutchouc', which comes from the Quechua
'kawchu'. It was the French who first introduced rubber
into Europe: Charles Marie de La Condamine sailed to South
America in 1736, and from Quito sent to the Académie Royale
des Sciences in Paris a long account of rubber, its uses and
production, as well as a small sample of the stuff.
Then, evidently enthused, in 1951 Condamine presented the
first ever scientific treatment of rubber to the Académie.

But the first use of this substance to erase pencil marks seems
to have occurred in England in the late 1700s. Prior to this
period, stale bread had been considered the optimum tool

for eliminating unwanted pencil lines. Then in 1770 Joseph Priestley wrote in his *Familiar Introduction to the Theory and Practice of Perspective* of 'a substance excellently adapted to the purpose of wiping from paper the marks of a black-lead-pencil', small cubes of which were sold by a certain Mr. Nairne, 'opposite the Royal Exchange', for the relatively high price of three shillings. Edward Nairne was better known in his lifetime as the inventor of the first maritime barometer, but his cubes of rubber soon became almost as widespread as the pencil itself, showing that trial and error, creation and correction, always go hand in hand. The name 'rubber' was coined because the substance rubs things out. In the US, and most of the world, they came to be known as 'erasers', and rubbers are something else.

The scientific principle of erasers is in reality very straightforward. A pencil works because graphite particles mingle with the fibre particles in the paper, particularly when pressure is applied. Erasers, conversely, are made up of polymers that are stickier than the paper fibres, and 'suck up' the graphite particles off the paper. Nairne's rubber, while

Image courtesy of Present & Correct

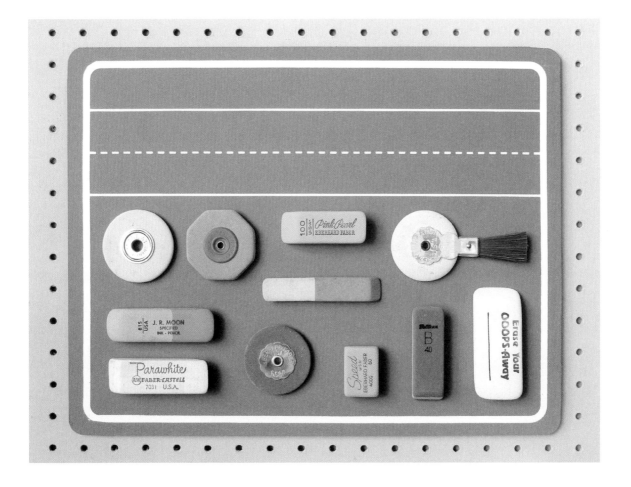

THE PINK PEARL

The Pink Pearl is, in many people's minds, the Platonic form of the eraser. Indeed, despite never having handled an eraser in their lives, many young people today will be familiar with it as the symbol used for the 'erase' tool on a range of design and illustration programs. But the Pink Pearl has been iconic for decades — between 1966 and '67, the Latvian-American artist Vija Celmins made a series of three sculptures of giant Pink Pearls (each one 11.2 feet long), as well as a pencil stub measuring 3 feet. But unlike Warhol's soup cans, for example, Celmins' erasers aren't symbols of mass production and consumption: their edges are well-worn, suggesting many mistakes made and rectified ('Change your mind as often as you like,' reads some early Pink Pearl ad copy).

The Pink Pearl went into production in 1916, taking its rather suggestive name from the Pearl Pencil that Eberhard Faber was producing at the time. Its gentle wedge shape was due to the fact that sharper corners tended to snap off during use, and were less comfortable in the palm, while its low price and reliability soon made it a classroom staple across the whole US. And generation after generation of schoolchildren have used them, cementing the Pink Pearl's place in American visual culture, its image appearing on everything from skateboards to nifty USBs.

And the Pink Pearl is still on sale today in an essentially unmodified form (there are not many products that remain as popular as they did 100 years ago). The difference is that today the eraser bears the name 'Papermate' — after a tortuous series of buyings, sellings and mergers, the product finally wound up in the possession of this stationery giant, who promptly stamped their name on it, as well as the legend 'latex-free'. Papermate have also launched a pair of ancillary products: the White Pearl and the Black Pearl (in a sort of pebble shape). We'll see if they're still around a century from now.

it will have been noticeably stickier that today's erasers, was rather erratic, and tended to smell bad after a while. So during the mid-1800s the American Charles Goodyear decided to work on rubber to make it more durable and chemically stable. Goodyear was the first to include sulphur in the mix, but unfortunately an Englishman called Hancock ripped him off and beat him to the patent for the 'vulcanization' process (Goodyear's name lives on in that of the tyre).

Hancock's vulcanized rubber was used in the 1858 patent issued to Hymen L. Lipman of Philadelphia, for a 'combination of lead-pencil and eraser' — the first incarnation of the modern, eraser-tipped pencil (interestingly, while the eraser-tip is the standard in the US, European pencils tend not to feature them).

In 1862, a Joseph Reckendorfer bought Lipman's patent for a not insignificant sum (as in Nairne's time, erasers clearly had a high profit margin) and began selling his own improvement on the model. The next twist in the rather backstabby story of the eraser came in 1875, when the pencil company Eberhard Faber started to sell their own rubber-tipped pencil. Suing them, Reckendorfer was told that both his and Lipman's patents were invalid, as they had not, in fact, invented something new, so much as combined two other things (in the account of the trial, the court compares their 'invention' to a screwdriver attached to the handle of a hammer). In the event, it was Eberhard Faber who went on to design what is for many the archetypal eraser: the Pink Pearl.

'Stale crumb of bread is better, if you are making a delicate drawing, than India-rubber, for it disturbs the surface of the paper less...' So wrote Ruskin in his *Elements of Drawing*, published in 1857 and identifying a problem that was to dog the eraser industries for decades to come: their coarseness, and their tendency to rub holes in the paper (Ruskin still came out in favour of the eraser, because the crumbs make a mess, and 'besides, you waste the good bread, which is wrong...'). It was as part of a search for a solution to this problem that during the following decades the eraser underwent a period of restlessness and self-improvement, giving rise to many variants on the same theme.

We saw that the polymers in the pure rubber used for the early erasers 'sucked up' the graphite of pencil marks. Modern erasers only contain about 20% natural or synthetic rubber, along with other ingredients including the 'factice', a mixture of vegetable or animal oil and sulphur, and

Opposite page: the Pink Pearl, familiar to generation upon generation of American schoolchildren; image courtesy of Present & Correct

abrasive materials such as pumice. Rubbing the eraser across the paper, these abrasives gently scratch the surface fibres of the paper, loosening the graphite particles, while the softeners help prevent the paper's tearing. Meanwhile, the heat generated by the friction of rubbing the eraser against the paper helps the rubber get sticky enough to hoover up graphite particles. This process produces small particles of graphite-suffused rubber that get left behind on the surface of the page, very much like the skid marks left behind by tyres on the tarmac. Other ingredients are used to affect the colour of the eraser — zinc oxide and titanium oxide can be combined to make white erasers, while red comes from iron oxide.

The ingredients of an eraser can be combined in various ways. Different compositions are more suited to different shapes and functions, and there is a panoply of different types, each one suited to a different context.

RUBBER ERASERS
Ask someone to visualise an eraser and, unless they are a member of the privileged fraternity of eraser fans, the classic rubber eraser shape is what'll pop into their head. The Pink Pearl is a rubber eraser, as are those found at the end of pencils. Generally made of a rubber and pumice mix, these erasers can be abrasive to the paper and smear or leave a residue.

Two geometric compositions of erasers. On the right, the colourful, ergonomic Koh-I-Noor hexagonal eraser; image courtesy of Present & Correct

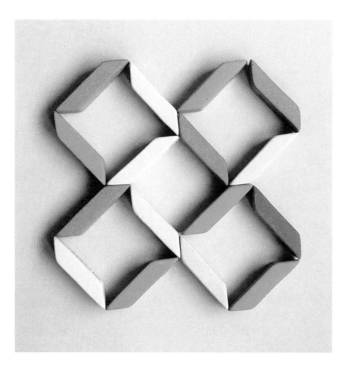

REPLAY PEN

Over the years, various erasers have been designed and marketed that purport to erase ink. As in the case of the typewriter eraser, however, what they do is use abrasion to remove the very top layer of paper, which holds the ink. There are, however, various tools and substances which do indeed erase ink, using scientific wizardry. Early products included the Sloan's Ink Eradicator, which involved the application of two chemicals to the page in succession, or the German-made Pelikan-Super-Pirat, a pen with two ends, one of which was an ink eradicator. These methods were only effective on royal blue fountain pen ink.

In the 1979, after ten years of development, Papermate launched the Replay pen (as it is known in Europe: in the US it is the Erasermate), which fast became an icon in the erasable ink world. The first Replays were refillable and looked a lot like an ordinary ball-point pen, albeit slightly chubbier. They featured a replaceable black eraser stuck to the cap, of roughly the same dimensions as a pencil-top eraser. The ink is slightly pressurized, meaning you can write on walls, or just about anything.

The unmistakable form of the Replay pen, pencil case staple for decades

VINYL ERASERS

First developed in the middle of the Twentieth Century, plasticized vinyl or, as they are known, plastic erasers, tend to be softer and cleaner than their rubber-based counterparts. Rather than absorbing the graphite, most of it is left in a vinyl residue that tends to clump together, making the rubbing process easier and cleaner. They are also less abrasive and thus popular with technicians and artists. Easily shaped, plastic is the preferred material for novelty erasers.

ART GUM

Made today from natural or synthetic rubber or vinyl, 'art gum' was originally trademarked in the US in 1907. Extremely soft, art gum crumbles on use, meaning that it never damages the paper, and all of the erased graphite impregnates the crumbles rather than the eraser itself. The copious residue has to be brushed or blown away with care, as it can make a mark.

KNEADED ERASERS
Popular with artists, the kneaded eraser can be moulded into a specific shape (a thin point, for example) or texture (like poster putty, which can be used in the same way, kneaded erasers can be used to remove only the top layer of a drawing, creating a shading effect). Good at removing both graphite and charcoal, kneading erasers absorb whatever they rub out, meaning that after a while the soiled exterior has to be kneaded inwards, hence the name.

CAP ERASERS
Often red or pink, these erasers are made to sit atop a pencil like a gnome's hat, solving the problem of the pencil-top eraser's getting worn down before the pencil does. They tend to be harder than other erasers to help them stay in place.

FIBREGLASS ERASERS
Generally a pen-shaped device that contains a replaceable tube of glass fibres. This is an extremely heavy-duty eraser, more commonly used to remove rust or clean circuit boards than erase pencil marks.

ELECTRIC ERASERS
Invented in 1932 by Albert J. Dremel, in Wisconsin, USA, the electric eraser features a replaceable cylinder held in place with a chuck driven by a small motor. The key concept is that the speed of rotation allows less pressure to be used, reducing abrasion on the paper. Modern electric erasers tend to feature a satisfyingly chunky handle and a fine, vinyl eraser tip.

TYPEWRITER ERASERS
Wandering in the Sculpture Garden of the National Gallery of Art in Washington, you may have come across a huge sculpture of a red disc sprouting what seem to be blue wires. This is a collaboration between Claes Oldenburg and Coosje van Bruggen, and depicts a giant typewriter eraser, which is why you may not have had any idea what it was. The typewriter eraser was born in the early Twentieth Century: it is particularly abrasive in order to erase the typewriter ink, and its thin disc shape enabled the user to erase one letter without touching any others. They often featured a long brush attachment, to remove any residue that might jam the mechanism.

PENCIL ERASERS

A pencil eraser is a pencil that, in place of graphite, features a particularly abrasive vinyl core that can be used to erase ink, essentially by scratching away the topmost layer of the paper. The A. W. Faber 'Perfection', finished in a pearly lacquer and often featuring a brush tip, is a classic in the genre.

CORRECTION FLUID

———————

Texas secretary Bette Nesmith Graham wasn't a very good typist, but she was able to rely on classic typewriter erasers to correct her mistakes — until, that is, her company brought in IBM electric typewriters in the 1950s, and she found that the ink they used would smear rather than disappear. Bette's eureka moment came when she was watching an artist hand-painting a sign: inspired, she put some tempera paint in a bottle, and brought it and her watercolour brush into work. This solution was highly effective and Bette decided to market her invention as 'Liquid Paper': by 1968, the company was producing 10,000 bottles a day (and Bette's son Mike, incidentally, had joined the Monkees). When the company was bought by the Gillette Corporation for a tidy sum in 1979, it was making over 25 million bottles every year.

In the US, correction fluid is just as likely to be known by the name of Liquid Paper. In Europe, it is often called 'Tipp-Ex', after one of the first brands to be marketed there. In fact, Tipp-Ex wasn't originally a correction fluid but a corrective tape that typists used to erase a mis-hit letter. When its creator Wolfgang Dabisch noted the success of Liquid Paper and similar products he determined to market his own, and did so with great success

— so much so that Tipp-Ex gave rise to its own verb, 'to tippex', a linguistic oddity, given that it comes from a combination of the German 'tippen', meaning to type, and Latin 'ex', meaning out.

Correction fluid dispensers have undergone various changes since the days of the bottle with the little brush, which is prone to spillage, and tends to ruin the brush: contemporary bottles instead feature a wedge-shaped sponge. Another solution was to do away with the bottle altogether, and replace it with a fat, squeezy pen with a metal nib. Then there is the Tipp-Ex Pocket Mouse, which dispenses a thin, papery tape when rolled over a mistake; a key advantage is that it may be written on directly, and by any type of writing implement.

CHOOSING KEEPING	
SHOP, STATIONERY	
London	U.K.

As one of the shop's curators explains, at Choosing Keeping, stationery is about more than pens and paper — it is a way of fighting back against the bland homogeneity of the digital world. Each object in the shop is charged with history, and its owners are recognized experts in the field, working as stationery consultants on major movies. Based in the vibrant East London borough of Hackney, Choosing Keeping is a favourite of the city's artists and designers, but also has a strong online presence. From their own line of wallets, to their extensive collection of pens and pencils, to beautiful desk objects, every item is a gem.

"Choosing Keeping was born, not as an exercise in branding or conceptual retail, but simply as a good old-fashioned shop, one that is personality-driven and constitutes a reflection of the owner's experience, knowledge, taste and interests — in this case, my own.

Part of what drives my selection is an invested interest in seeing industry — from the artisanal to the mass-manufactured — survive in Europe, and by extension in other fully industrialised countries. Mainly I believe that everyday functional objects can be considered to be as much of a national cultural icon as a painting hanging in a museum. The four-

Previous spread and below: the characterful interior of the store, showing many of the rare and beatiful stationery items on sale

colour ballpoint Bic pen, the Clairefontaine French cahier and its tablecloth design, or the Japanese wax Sakura Coupy-pencil are all examples of things which hold deep sentimental meaning for me, as treasures of my childhood which I seek to assemble in the form of Choosing Keeping. My goal is share the wonder of all these nostalgic objects which we often take for granted and could easily disappear.

It is not environmental conservation — it's industrial conservation.

We see a wide-ranging group of people coming through our doors. Due to our location we have a solid customer base in the creative field — architects, artists, fashion designers, art dealers, illustrators, photographers and generally creative professionals are all regulars at our shop. I particularly enjoy working with set designers who need to source pens and bits for period films. Because we do quite a bit of research for each piece of stationery we stock (where and when it was first made, for example) we are able to advise on historical accuracy. This is something I love doing, as it puts my

knowledge to the test and it is lovely to see our stationery in finished films. Often we go to the cinema to spot the props, naming brands of pens and pencils seen in films.

Talking to customers gives me a chance to explain the selection of items the shop carries. In the first year, this selection was very 'easy' to make, and personal — I collected all the bits I had loved and missed from my own childhood. I travelled a lot as a child in Asia and Europe and this made for an interesting and fresh selection of exotic products. Thankfully, as a natural-born collector I had carefully kept all my possessions from decades past, and so had a great box of samples to work with.

Now that we have become a stationery specialist store, our selection is the result of a much more complex research process, which includes customer recommendations, travel, looking for stationery in films, talking to suppliers, old stationery catalogues, etc. I majored in history so you could say I take an academic approach to our selection. Indeed, the idea that objects are pieces of history is very much the foundation and premise of Choosing Keeping. All the items we sell are great starting points to discuss social history, art history, manufacturing history, war history, and so on. If you look at the Japanese items we offer, for example, together they say a lot about Twentieth Century Japan, especially the period

Some of the vintage fountain
and ball-point pens available

of rapid modernisation that the country went through in the Meiji Restoration.

An example of this is the ballpoint pen in a wooden barrel which was in 1949 the first ballpoint pen to be manufactured in the country. This was a Japanese pastiche of Reynolds ballpoint pens brought in by American GIs in post-war Japan. It's an example of how American culture filtered into Japanese everyday life.

Another, more poignant, example of stationery as history is the gem paper clip which was worn on jacket lapels by Norwegians during World War II as a symbol of resistance and solidarity against the German occupiers.

I consider our shop to be a mini-museum of present-day objects which really ought to have a place in a museum archive, as documentation of pre-1980s, Twentieth Century life. I love to find that special something at the back of a shop, or the back of a catalogue of a forgotten and unloved supplier — it's about discovery, or re-discovery! For example, this year I am finally getting round to having some packaging made, but this only came about because I happened, through an obscure trade grapevine, to find out about a small traditional supplier, unlisted on the internet. I like it when things happen like this, in a spontaneous way. It's like finding treasure.

As a fountain pen user (probably the only real piece of stationery I use daily) I would say that the Yellow Lamy Safari is very special to me. I've owned the same one for 20 years. I love the company's approach to business — embracing modernity without compromising on its vision. They have to be one of the easiest suppliers to deal with from a logistics point of view. I think this clarity and organisation carries through into their products. Things work and have become design classics because generations of children have used them daily — as well as professionals (especially architects). The Lamy Safari which was born in 1980 follows Bahaus principles — my only wish is that they would go back to making it with the black clip.

Regarding people who only collect stationery — I would say that it isn't collecting. It is some form of consumerism, comparable to how some people can't help but buy cosmetics beyond their needs and have bathrooms full of perfumes. Pinterest and online obsessions with stationery are not something I can comment on. It is not what Choosing Keeping is about.

The paperless office is a myth. Pens and paper are still essential in the developing of ideas and thinking — most brains need a physicality in the creative process. Pen and paper offers something quite different to computers, and so they can live in harmony, because they are not mutually substitutable, at least not completely. We have sent out many orders to Silicon Valley addresses.

There are two elements which I believe are key to under-standing why stationery still holds such power. The first is nostalgia: stationery is a low-tech time travel device to childhood, a time which is for many filled with precious memories of places and people. Like Proust's madeleines, stationery can instantly revive treasured memories.

And the second is what I call the blank slate effect: new pens and fresh notebooks allow for a sense of re-invention. Half way between OCD and procrastination, stationery creates the mental space in which one can project one's dreams of organisation and efficiency. I often stress to customers, however, that it is important not to get stuck in that vision of perfect tools, but rather to consider stationery functionally, and make creation and action their priorities."

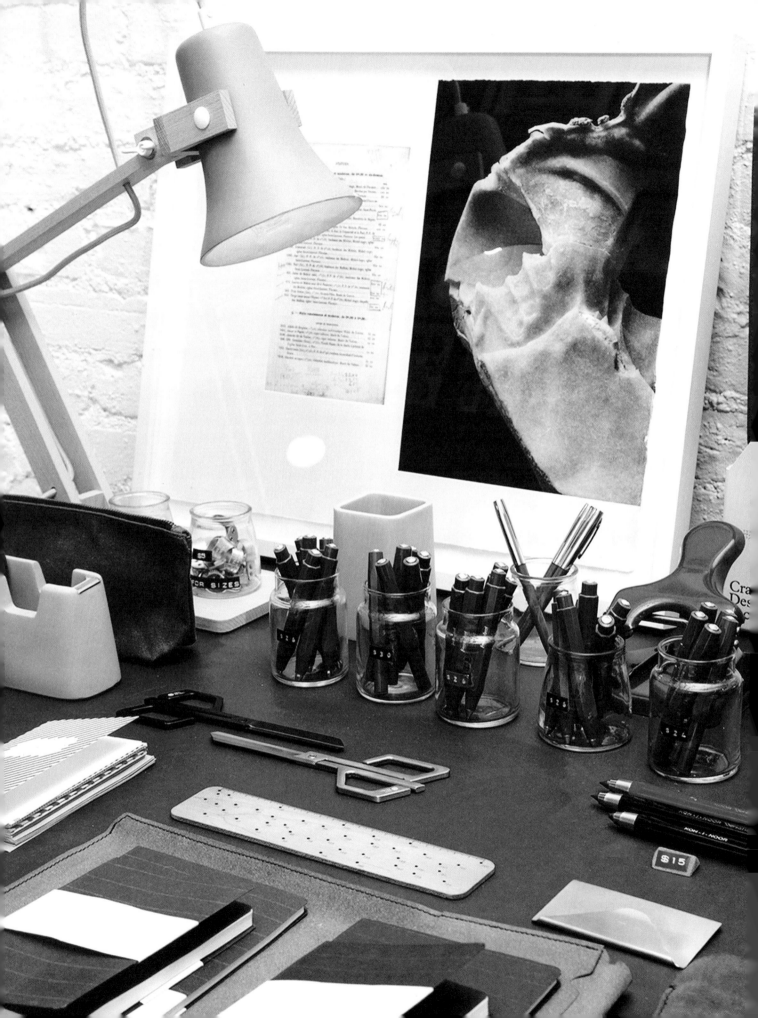

```
┌─────────────────────────────────┐
│          MC NALLY               │
│          JACKSON                │
├─────────────────────────────────┤
│       SHOP, STATIONERY          │
├──────────────────┬──────────────┤
│    New York      │    U.S.A      │
└──────────────────┴──────────────┘
```

MC NALLY JACKSON

SHOP, STATIONERY

New York	U.S.A

We can see how seriously stationery is taken at the McNally Jackson Store by the fact that its website features a quote from Ralph Waldo Emerson, urging readers to 'build your own world' and 'conform your life to the pure idea in your mind'. To do so, you need look no further than their collection of pure, elegant, sometimes austere, stationery and furniture. Curated by Sandeep Kaur Salter and team, Goods for the Study is located in the heart of Manhattan and at the cutting edge of design — the ideal place to start building your own world, one fountain pen at a time.

"Goods for the Study sells objects that support the life of the mind, from pens and notebooks, to desks and lighting. We believe that the right tools and objects can truly enrich one's study practice. There is something for everybody in the store: we strive to stock a diverse range of products that will appeal to people from all walks of life. Mostly our customers tend to be people who regularly engage in writing or drawing. I hope we draw individuals who are thoughtful about the objects they fill their life with, and knowing many of our customers, I think we do.

An aspect of that is that no one who shops with us is just buying these things as a pastime. If anything, using physical drawing

Below: the enticing shopfront

and writing implements has become much more significant to people's process because it re-engages them with the tactility of their work. The value of paper, pens, pencils, and so on, is in their usefulness and necessity. We aren't just selling beautiful letter writing sets that fulfil some sense of nostalgia — we're selling materials for everyday life, for people who go through stacks of sketchpads each year, who have countless to-do lists, or who carry a pen in their pocket just in case.

We take inspiration from all over the place. Traveling is a big part of it — we recently found some incredible items in Japan and Italy. We are always looking, and always asking the people we know what they use and love. We only stock items that are useful and beautiful. If something doesn't work properly, or its mechanism is awkward, then it has no place in our store. Quite simply, if the object is useful for one's study practice, or has a place on one's desk, then it has a place in our store. Many of our biggest sellers embody this philosophy: the Midori Brass pen, Craft Design Technology Tradio Plastic Fountain Pen, Solid Manufacturing Leather Document Cases, Blackwing Pencils.

Most of the objects we sell tell a story, more often than not about their maker. For example, we have beautiful hand-forged brass and maple letter openers made in a small town in Japan — each one is unique and has been made with great care. The pen line Tetzbo is made by an individual artisan in Tokyo who assembles custom-welded ballpoint pens using pipes and other mechanical materials. We also sell leather pieces handmade by Andrey and Shay, a young artist duo who work in Tel Aviv, making incredible conceptual art and design projects, as well as a line of beautiful leather goods. A pair of scissors by Craft Design Technology were manufactured in Gifu, Japan, in a small factory known for making samurai swords. The stories go on and on. I have strong relationships with all of our suppliers and I respect them all immensely for what they do.

Right and below: parts of the store are laid out to resemble a desk or office space

Goods for the Study celebrates the materiality
of stationery, encouraging customers to
reconnect with the physical side of creativity

I personally collect artwork, but with my stationery I am very selective; I don't like to have too much. I have two very special pens, a gold Sailor Chalana Fountain pen and a Brass Tetzbo Ballpoint Pen that I use at home for writing. I also have a number of antique tools that are rather dear to me: an ivory and brass folding ruler and a jade sharpener that my husband gave to me in particular are very beautiful.

I'm quite sure there have always been people obsessed with stationery. Right now, stationery garners a lot of attention or fetishisation because it's sort of pinned up as an alternative to the digital, and I don't really think it needs to be so black and white. I do think that people find that they can re-connect to their work process using these tools, and incorporating them into their work life can be very rewarding. There is a meaningfulness in taking pen to paper that cannot necessarily be duplicated by any digital experience, and so I suppose people want to celebrate that."

CHAPTER Nº4

PEN

Writing with ink
through the ages

'I observed that it was a wonderful piece of work, the like of which I had never imagined I would ever see.' Writing in the Tenth Century, Islamic chronicler Qadi Noman was overcome by awe at the world's first fountain pen: 'behold, it turned out to be a pen which can be turned upside down in the hand and tipped from side to side, and no trace of ink appears from it.' Qadi Noman was even moved to extrapolate 'a fine moral example' from it, in that the pen 'lavishes benefits on whoever seeks them, but withholds them from the person who does not thus seek; and because of what it contains within itself, it is independent of any outside assistance'.

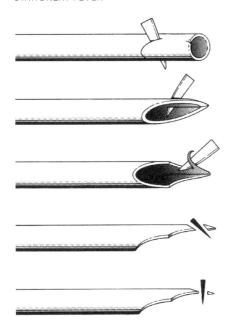

Although he does not supply any technical stats, Qadi Noman's description is the first record we have of a pen that contained a reservoir of ink. His wonderment is comprehensible, when we take into account that for several thousand years before him (not to mention several hundred after), all pens worked on a dipping principle, and were in other words entirely reliant on the close proximity of a bottle of ink.

In his authoritative *History of Writing*, Steven Roger Fischer explains how two approaches to writing emerged in the ancient world, one in Mesopotamia, based on clay tablets, and another in Ancient Egypt that used papyrus. While in Mesopotamia, lines and symbols were pressed into wet clay, in Egypt papyrus was written on with ink and a pen made from a reed or thin stick of bamboo. Often featuring a split nib, examples of these pens have been found at sites dating to the Fourth Century BC, and they endured in one form or another well into the Medieval era. (It is thought that it is thanks to the fact it made use of pen and ink, rather than cumbersome clay, that Egyptian writing is at the root of many modern alphabet systems.)

In the European Middle Ages, parchment became the medium of choice, and its smooth surface allowed for finer, smaller writing, giving rise in turn to the invention of the quill pen. Quills were made from the wing feathers of, usually, geese (feathers from the left wing of the bird were favoured by the right-handed majority of scribes, as the quill curves out of the way over the back of the right hand). The feather was then buried in hot sand, to make it less brittle, and the flights removed (most medieval scribes' quills looked more like shaved sticks, and the full ostrich plume pen is a Hollywood fantasy). The thicker tip was carved with a pen knife into a nib that was split up the middle, as the stylus was and as modern fountain pens are. The hollow shaft of the feather served as a reservoir, and ink flowed to the tip via capillary action.

Above: cutting a quill requires certain skill. A how-to guide in five steps

Below: an illustration of the correct way to hold and write with a quill pen

The quill pen remained the writing implement of choice in the Western world for more than a thousand years — everything from the Domesday Book to the Declaration of Independence was written with one. In fact, metal-based alternatives (in other words, nibs) had been known since Pompeii, and Samuel Pepys, irrepressible gadget lover, mentions 'a silver pen to carry ink in'. But it was not until the Industrial Revolution that metallurgy had advanced sufficiently to produce a nib that was fine and flexible enough to be written with, and only in 1822 did metal pens begin seriously to be promoted as an alternative to quills, when John Mitchell of Birmingham

began to sell mass-produced pens with metal nibs. By 1850, Birmingham was producing more than half the world's nibs.

These pens featured a steel nib set in a handle, often made of wood. Today called dip or nib pens, their low cost made them popular in educational settings well into the Twentieth Century — dip pens continue to be popular with artists and illustrators for the technical possibilities they offer. Using the same technique as a quill pen, dip pens can be used with any type of ink, including those as would ruin a fountain pen. And they are much more sensitive to modulations of speed or pressure, making a line that can be more reminiscent of that of a paintbrush. The great variety of nibs together offer the dip pen user an enviably wide range of possibilities.

But nib pens did not have much of a chance to get a foothold in the market, as the fountain pen was first patented in 1827. The pen described by Qadi Noman, as well as a 1636 design featuring a quill pen with another 'reservoir' quill inside it, show that the idea of a pen that could carry and administer its own supply of ink was not a ground-breaking one. What was lacking were the technological smarts to produce more than costly and

Above: a box of Trionfo nibs, produced in Italy

Below: some rare nib holders with calligraphy nibs from the collection of Orlando Vallucci

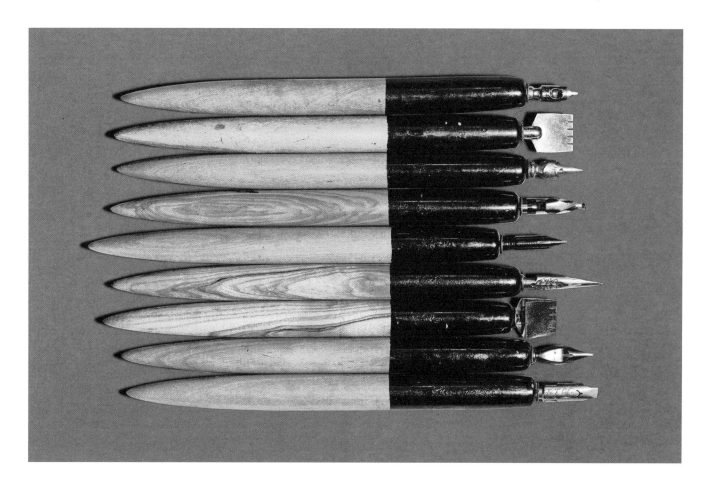

Some rare nibs and their original boxes
from the collection of Orlando Vallucci

Opposite: The incredible variety
of designs makes them a treat for
collectors around the world, also from
the collection of Orlando Vallucci

erratic prototypes. The first fountain pen (creation of Romanian inventor Petrache Poenaru) still featured a large swan quill, and it took decades of blue sky thinking to arrive at something resembling, in form and functionality, its modern incarnation.

What was most problematic about the earliest fountain pens was the refilling process. Almost all models featured an unscrewable portion, which was filled with ink from an eyedropper. This was a tedious and messy procedure, and made fountain pens very prone to leakage. It was replaced with the 'self filler', which worked on the basis of a rubber sac that was used to suck ink up into the cartridge that sat inside the pen. A flurry of increasingly ornate filling mechanisms proliferated in the Twentieth Century (among them the Pelikan screw mechanism, which sucked ink up through the nib into a piston), until Waterman introduced the disposable plastic cartridge in the '50s, thereby setting a standard that endures to this day.

There are of course enough makers and different types of fountain pen to fill numerous volumes. However, we can trace the story of the pen's development by concentrating on a few iconic brands. The early history of the fountain pen is bound up in particular with Lewis Edson Waterman and the company that took his name. Born in 1837, Waterman was a New York insurance salesman: according to Waterman corporate guff, after a faulty pen blotted an important contract, he was moved to invent a fountain pen that released a uniform flow of ink. The solution he devised, known as the feed, remains in various different forms a standard feature on fountain pens. The first Waterman pens also used 14 carat gold nibs, now prized by collectors. The Waterman heyday occurred around the turn of the Twentieth Century, and endured until the '30s, when competitors like Parker and Sheaffer began to outpace them. Waterman in the US shut down in 1954, but its French wing continued to do business, and was shuffled around between different stationery conglomerates before ending up in the hands of Newell Rubbermaid.

Waterman's rival the Parker Pen Company was founded in 1888 by George Safford Parker, who got his first patent in 1889 for the 'Lucky Curve' feed, an improvement on the basic Waterman design. From the 1920s to the dawn of the ballpoint, Parker was consistently either the biggest or second biggest writing implement brand in the world. In 1931, it invented Quink, a quick drying ink that removed the need for blotting (prior to this, after writing a letter with a fountain pen, it was necessary to press it ink-side-down on a sheet of thick, absorbent blotting paper; blotting pads served as writing surfaces). And Parker was responsible for the most iconic of

The stainless steel nib of the 1939
Montblanc Meisterstück 138, from
the collection of Christof Zollinger

fountain pens, the Parker 51. Another brand sucked up by
Newell Rubbermaid in the late Twentieth Century, Parker
today concentrates on the high-end fountain pen market.

Like so many innovators in the stationery world, Walter A.
Sheaffer was the classic rags-to-riches early American dreamer
— his first job was as a printer's devil, which was surely a lowly
post, whatever it entailed. In 1913, he used his life savings to
set up Sheaffer pens following his invention of a lever-based
pen-filling device that, in the words of the company literature,
'fills instantly from any ink-well, with one touch of a finger'.
The Sheaffer company was at the forefront of innovations in
filling mechanisms until 1959, when it got on-board with
plastic ink cartridges. In the same year it introduced its 'Inlaid
Nib', which remains a distinctive feature on its high-end pens.
Bought by Bic in 1997, in 2008 Sheaffer's fountain pen plant was
outsourced to China, and in 2014 it was bought by the A. T. Cross
Company for all of 15 million dollars.

The drawn-out, inglorious demises of the fountain pen giants
are, of course, attributable to the dawn of the ball-point
pen. And in this story, too, we come across similar figures:
industrious immigrants, startling technological innovations,
and much backstabbing and pipping to the post.

PARKER 51

Launched in 1941, the Parker 51 was an innovative de-sign, with its body made of Lucite (a thermoplastic used in submarine periscopes, among other things), its tip of Plathenium (a platinum/ruthenium alloy), and a 14 karat gold nib fitted inside a hood, making it 'a pen that won't flood, leak or sweat' as some early publicity put it.

A canny wartime marketing campaign guaranteed that, once restrictions were lifted on materials following the war, the 51 became a huge hit. László Moholy-Nagy, who later worked for Parker, characterized it as 'one of the most successful designs of small utility objects in our period', and it has been voted the fourth best piece of industrial design from the Twentieth Century.

A selection of vintage pens featuring the so-called 'hooded nib', showing the influence of the Parker 51 on other makers' designs

Below: second generation 1948 Parker 51 pencil and fountain pen set (in the uncommon Nassau Green colour) in their original clam shell box, also from the collection of Christof Zollinger

FLOATY PEN

A familiar sight in tourist gift shops and promotional goody bags the world over, the floaty pen features a plastic case rather like an elongated goldfish bowl that contains a special oil mix, within which an object slides when the pen is tilted one way or the other: a vaporetto crosses a miniature Venice; an elephant traverses a savannah; a couple are locked in a never-ending game of ping pong. The first floaty pens were made by the Eskesen Company in the 1950s. Eskesen was set up by Peder Eskesen in 1946, in a town about an hour outside Copenhagen, Denmark.

A driving force in the development of keychain ornaments, it was with the 'floating action pen' that Eskesen really established their presence in the novelty stationery market. One of the more common applications of the floaty pen has always been for promotional purposes. Eskesen's first commission was for Esso, and featured an oil barrel sliding up and down in clear oil. Since then, the company has produced a wide range of takes on its classic 534 model, most notably for the 1996 Atlanta Olympics. Other designs, known as 'tip and strips', involve a model whose clothes slide off at the slightest provocation.

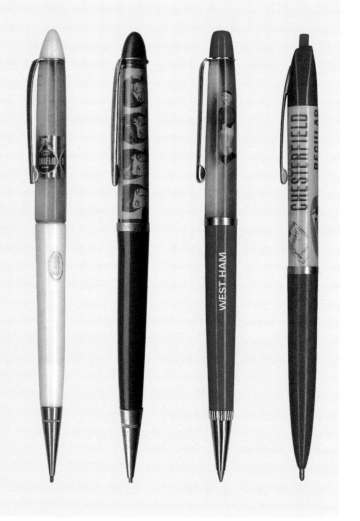

Born in Budapest in 1899, Lázló Bíró was, among other things, a surrealist painter, the first person to introduce the study of hypnosis in Hungary, and the inventor of the automatic gearbox. It was while working as a journalist that he first decided to create a pen that worked with the same quick-drying ink as was used for newspaper print. Being highly viscous, however, this ink didn't work in fountain pens, so Bíró collaborated with his brother on the chemistry behind it, and they showcased their prototype at the 1931 Budapest World Fair.

A fortuitous meeting with the former president of Argentina led to the Bíró brothers fleeing there from Nazi Germany and setting up a company to manufacture their pen. It was an instant hit, but the Bírós had run out of money for further R&D. Enter Henry George Martin, a British-born entrepreneur

who in 1944 bought 51% of the nascent company (can you tell where this is going?). Martin went ahead and signed deals with various international big fish, among them Eversharp/Eberhard Faber, which in 1946 launched the Eversharp CA pen, based on the capillary action developed by Bíró.

In the UK, in 1945 the Miles Martin Pen Company started selling refillable ball-point pens as Biros. The Biro was a revolutionary product, but at over two pounds (that is, more than a secretary's weekly wage) it was far from an office essential. Enter Marcel Bich, an Italian baron who in 1950 bought the patent from Bíró and started churning out super cheap Bic pens, to which range he was soon to add disposable lighters and disposable razors, making the Bic company a pioneer in high volume, low cost mass production. As his obituary in the *Independent* put it, '[I]f the mass-market had a patron saint it would be Bich: for mere pennies the ordinary man can write more clearly, shave more closely and have more reliable access to fire than a renaissance prince.' There followed a period of extended legal wrangling between the Bic and Biro imprints, with Bic eventually gaining the upper hand and in 1957 acquiring 47% of shares in Biro Swan Ltd., as it was then known. In a rather Byzantine twist, the son of Henry George Martin, the man responsible for commercializing Bíró's design, ended up marrying Baron Bich's daughter Caroline. Bíró himself never made a lot of money and worked in the latter part of his life as a consultant in an Argentine pen company. Argentine Inventors' Day is held on his birthday, though, which is something.

This page: period Bic advertising from France, alongside a close-up of the immortal design that made it famous

THE SPACE PEN

It is a shame the story isn't true, as it seems to illustrate some essential point about human ingenuity. Nonetheless, a pencil is obviously the wrong sort of instrument to have on board a spaceship, given that snapped leads and bits of wood flying around the place would obviously constitute a serious hazard, and the urban myth about how the Americans spent millions on developing a space pen that would write upside down, only to find that the Soviet astronauts were using pencils, is thus exactly that: a myth.

The space pen was in fact developed by entrepreneur Paul C. Fisher, inventor of the universal pen refill. In 1965 he invited NASA to try out his design, and they duly ended up buying 400 for use in the Apollo missions (the Soviets also bought some). The science of the pen is reasonably straightforward: a compressed nitrogen gas forces the ink out of the cartridge at a pressure of around 40 pounds per square inch. This action requires a special kind of viscoelastic ink, which is thick and rubbery until the shearing action of the rolling ball liquefies it. This combination of elements allows you to write in a range of unorthodox settings, among them zero gravity, and from any angle you like.

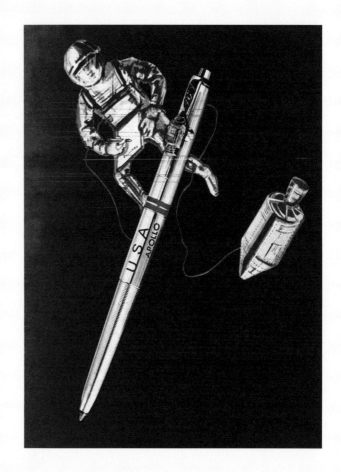

Some period advertising for the Fisher space pen from the era of the Moon Landings

WHY NASA SELECTED the Fisher Space Pen

LA PENNA SPAZIALE

Desidero ricevere LA PENNA A SFERA SPAZIALE adottata dalla « NASA », e in dotazione agli ASTRONAUTI completa di certificato di GARANZIA di origine della Fisher Pen Company, Illinois che ne garantisce l'originalità.

Qualora la penna non fosse in perfetto ordine la ritornerò a: STUDIO 1 - Via Moscova 40/6 20121 MILANO, per la sostituzione senza alcuna ulteriore spesa.

I. P.

LA PENNA DEGLI ASTRONAUTI

STACCARE

da questo

inserto

La CARTOLINA da compilare

In the US, ball-point technology took a while to take off — the opportunistic Reynold's International Pen Company put out a highly faulty range, and the Eversharp ballpoint did not live up to expectations. By the '50s the ball-point boom had receded, and the Reynolds company went under. This cleared the way for new entries in the field, chief among them Paper Mate, who pioneered new ink formulas, which it promoted as being 'banker-approved'. Then in 1954 Parker put out the Jotter, their second ball-point, that featured a plunger and stainless steel cap, as well as tungsten-carbide ball-bearings. They sold several million in the space of a year, and the Jotter remains one of Parker's flagship products, with over 750 million sold worldwide (Eversharp threw in the towel in the '60s and sold out to Parker).

Pelikan India ink set from c. 1950

Ink is an infinitely varied and interesting world. It was the Chinese, of course, who first discovered how to make India ink, in the middle of the Third Millennium BCE. Gutenberg's invention of the printing press sparked a revolution in ink-making — the oil based formula Gutenberg came up with is the forefather of modern inks

The next big step forward in the pen world was the rollerball. Launched in 1963 by pioneering Japanese pen and ink company Ohto, the rollerball pen was designed to combine the familiar ease of the ball-point with a fountain pen's 'wet ink' effect. Like fountain pens, the rollerball uses a water-based ink that is less viscous than the oil-based inks used in ball-point. This means that is it more easily absorbed and enables the pen to move more smoothly across the surface of the paper.

A variant on the rollerball is the gel pen, first produced by the Japanese Sakura Color Products Corporation in 1984, which uses an ink composed of pigment suspended in a water-based gel. Although rollerballs generally write for much less time than a ball-points, the gel pen in particular is a popular product, partly thanks to the thick, characterful line it leaves, and the fact that the gel can be made to hold glittery particles and suchlike. And that, in truth, is pretty much where the pen market stands today. While a nice Parker or Montblanc continues to bestow an aura of culture and wealth on its user, and the biro remains a more or less necessary bit of office stationery, the pen will never regain the ubiquity it enjoyed last century. Nevertheless, in its many different incarnations, it remains a useful and valued tool, as well as a prized collectible. The pen isn't going anywhere.

The Pen Store, based in Stockholm, Sweden, and run by Alice Myr and Jacob Bergström, is one of the world's only shops dedicated exclusively to the mighty pen. This single-minded focus is reflected in its sleek, spotless grey interiors, housing rank upon rank of every pen imaginable: 'markers, fountain pens, mechanical pencils, brush-tip pens' and more.

"A love for stationery seems to me to be a natural reaction to the modern way of life, a need for something time-consuming. We believe the pen is at the core of creativity. It's impossible for technology to pull the carpet out from under the feet of something that essential.

Our store is dedicated to the pen: the fountain pen, the marker pen, and the office pen one of your colleagues will sooner or later steal. Sure, we like paper goods and nice stationery — but for us they're just accessories to the pen. That's what it all sprung from.

In our shop we mix strong brands with hard-to-find specialty products. For us, one of the keys to success has been to bring in wide ranges of high-demand products, and at the same time research those special items. It makes for a very nice mix. The playful Lamy Safari fountain pen, the classic Rotring mechanical pencil, and the Swedish Ballograf ballpoint pen

Previous and current spreads: the sleek, stark,
stylish shopfront and interiors showcase
a breathtaking range of pens

are some of the most popular products in our shop.
Our typical customer is unpretentious and values good
quality products. The perfect customer has actively chosen
us — whether it's for our knowledge, assortment, prices or
something else. In terms of what we stock, with pens and
pencils, there's very few limitations. Our other products,
however, should have a direct connection to the use of pens.

I am a heavy user but not a collector of stationery. But even a
minimalistic and unsentimental pen salesman as myself has a
few items too special to let go. One of my favourite products is
the Lamy 2000 fountain pen. It's such a timeless piece. It was
designed in 1966, but could easily have been produced today.
Bauhaus design at its best. It's just very hard to beat.

We're mainly an online retailer and want our customers to experience that seamless shopping where online and offline just float together. The physical store is a great way for us to meet our customers — but the online store is an irreplaceable method of reaching out. We run a dynamic shop and try to be responsive to our customers' needs."

PRESENT & CORRECT

SHOP, PRODUCER	
London	U.K.

With its Islington location, Present & Correct is at the heart of London's design hub. James Ward, author of *Adventures in Stationery*, called it 'the most wonderful stationery shop in London', and, browsing its shelves or online catalogue, it's easy to see why. Present & Correct carries a range of vintage paper products from around the world, as well as many contemporary iconic items. Curator Neal Whittington goes on four sourcing trips each year, and his unique vision is evident in the gorgeous presentation of the shop's stock.

"The concept of Present & Correct is really very simple: it's a store that sells stationery and desktop equipment we love. We wanted it to feel like a sweet shop for office supplies! A mixture of old and new, and our own designs, it was always important that the stock change often, and that we only sell items which we would want to own ourselves.

I think our taste ties the new and the old together, because we have a very graphic approach — so whatever their age, the products almost look as if they are all from the same place. It also helps that we style our photos, because that ties them together in a similar aesthetic. We do our best to stick with office supplies, which means everything from erasers to desk trays and boxes (we love storage!). Occasionally we deviate, but we do our best not to. I think that in this day and age, when people work from home and the idea of an office is more fluid, what 'stationery' encompasses is a little broader, but the essentials are still the same as they have always been.

The bottom line is that the collection reflects our taste — it's just things we find attractive and appealing. And that's a hard thing to pinpoint sometimes. I've always liked forms and postal ephemera, stamps, mid-century type and foreign packaging. Also I really like everyday materials or objects looked at in a new way, and also products which reference something else. A general interest in design and trends informs everything.

Previous and current spreads: a selection of the beautiful compositions that make the shop's marketing so distinctive

I love styling our products; it's really fun, and a nice creative thing to do on a weekly basis. I think its hugely important to present your products in a way that is different to everyone else, as it unifies them and gives them a character. There are so many online stores now, and by styling your products you can create a brand look and feel, something which develops over time and becomes recognisable to customers. I'm a strong believer in companies having personality and humour; it can still look great without being po-faced.

We ran the website for several years before opening the store, and it is still the main business, because we ship all over the world. The advantage of being online is that it brings people to the store, so a presence on social media helps to make people aware of the retail space. I definitely think that the relationship is symbiotic: the digital presence of P & C is as enjoyable as the physical version, just in a different way.

Our customer base is really varied. I would say we have a lot of graphic designers, architects, and artists, too. There is a mixture of all age groups, all with their love of stationery in common. It's been lovely having an actual retail space because we get to meet customers face to face. The people who visit us are so supportive, kind and interested. We feel lucky to have such nice people visit us daily.

Our biggest sellers vary all the time: vintage stock always does very well because it is unique and you can't find it everywhere. We work hard to stock things which other people don't have in the UK, and whatever that item is will do well because it has not been seen anywhere else. Gridded items are always popular, as are products featuring solid blocks of colour or letters. There really isn't a stand-out, which I am pleased about because it's nice that our customers like the variety that we stock.

Part of P & C's success comes from the fact we love doing this and have fun with it. You can't fake an enthusiasm for something; it's so important to love what you do. In fact, the shop feels like an extension of my collection, I am amongst it every day and so

Some of the rare and vintage
paper stationery on sale

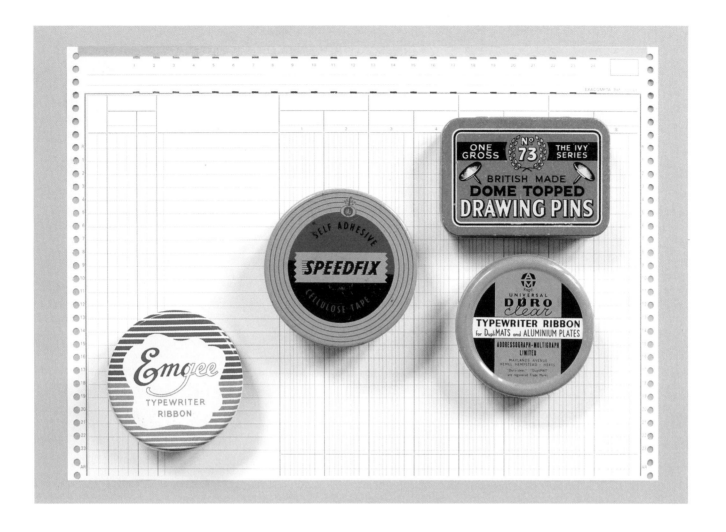

feel like I own it — even though any of it could be bought at any moment. I love that the stock changes a lot: the collection never gets boring. Some things I will keep longer than others, because I want to feel like I own them for a little while, and if I find a lot of a particular item I might keep one for myself. And I record everything with photos and also scan a lot of books and ephemera.

Even the smallest vintage label is evocative of an earlier time. I love that something throwaway can tell us so much about how things have changed. Like old price tickets from shops, to food labels or invoice books. Items which were once a very normal, everyday thing but now seem quite unusual.

There has definitely been a surge of interest in stationery in recent years and I think it comes back to our world being dominated by screens and the digital — stationery offers the opposite of that. It's also a comforting nostalgia for our generation, who grew up with traditional materials at school, before computers took over. So it harks back to that too.

Also stationery can be an affordable treat, something which is useful and attractive that doesn't break the bank. Stationery can make you feel inspired, organised and prepared and all of those things put together are a good thing.

People will always like objects which are rare or unique. So that's another level of the appeal. Also the old items are not like today's: they have a different aesthetic and the materials are different, so that too is something which people like. A lot of aspects of life have become homogenised and vintage items offer an alternative to that. They feel special in many ways, yet are still useful.

Collecting is never a waste of time. If you like something enough to collect it then that is a good enough reason. I think humans will always like physical things; we are tactile creatures. And although we are all on computers every day, I think that is more of a reason to seek out real books, real pens and paper. Just as small-time manufacturers have became revered again, as an antithesis to the mass-produced, I think that traditional writing materials are going the same way, because we are saturated with technology and the digital. Human habits are cyclical I think, and when we have too much of something we strive for the opposite."

Present & Correct embodies an approach to stationery that combines the vintage and the contemporary. Form and function are balanced in these sumptuous items

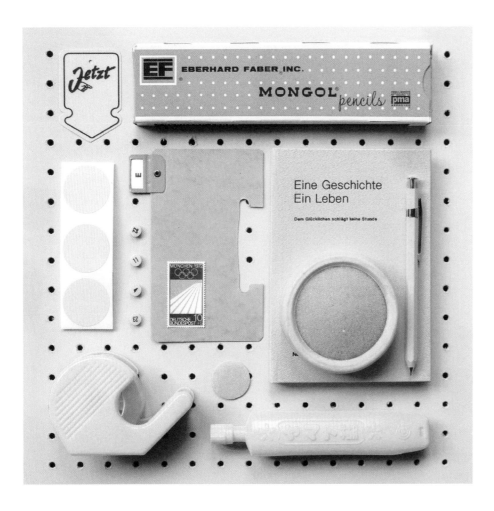

CHAPTER Nº5

NOTEBOOK

Seedbed of ideas
and to-do lists

Paper is history and technology. Paper stands for writing, reading and learning, for communication and information. It is how the dead talk to us, and how we talk to them. In a word, paper is civilization, and the history of paper from its invention in Ancient China, through its uptake by the Arabic and European nations (as well as its parallel discovery in pre-Colombian America), is in many senses a history of culture, of ideas and how they spread.

FIELD NOTES
Set up in 2007, Field Notes have fast become an iconic notebook brand. Designed to look like the promotional notebooks given to farmers by tractor companies in the 1920s, they are made to be carried and used in any situation

CUADERNOS (N.1, 2, 3, 4)
This collection of four notebooks designed by Jaime Narváez for Belleza Infinita proposes new patterns drawn from traditional lines and squares. They can be seen as drawings, even though they maintain their functionality as a conventional notebook, and thus return our gaze to the medium itself

Here, what we are interested in is paper in its virgin state, when it represents nothing but pure potential. 'The pages are still blank,' wrote Vladimir Nabokov, 'but there is a miraculous feeling of the words being there, written in invisible ink and clamouring to become visible.' Until a handful of years ago, ideas were only ideas once they had entered into contact with a piece of paper. 'The blank page gives the right to dream,' as Gaston Bachelard put it, and the legacy of many of the world's greatest writers and creators is indistinguishable from the blank pieces of paper they used to dream on — Leonardo da Vinci, for example, or Charles Darwin, or Emily Dickinson in her homemade 'fascicle' notebooks.

In 1914, the Italian Girolamo Moretti published his fascinating, bonkers *Manual of Graphology*, which contains many tips for evaluating someone's character based on their handwriting. One of these tips is to study the direction of the lines — if they are angled upwards, he says, they show you are arrogant and domineering, while lines that slant downwards suggest a tendency to depression. Don't worry, though, if you are a closet megalomaniac, as there is an easy way to throw sleuthing graphologists off your tracks: lined notepaper will keep your handwriting neatly aligned and your psychopathology under wraps.

Although there was a time when a feature of classroom note-taking involved using a ruler to draw in the lines yourself, today most notebooks for students feature faint, equidistant lines running horizontally across the surface of each page, intended to guide the handwriting and give rise to neatly ordered rows of words. As it happens, this feature is almost as old as the blank piece of paper itself. In the Middle Ages, lead was used to rule lines on parchment, to ensure that the text of a manuscript was uniform, while in a Sixteenth Century writing manual we read that a piece of paper had to be scored with 'parallel lines marked with the tin stylus or a pen knife'.

Then in 1667 Edward Cocker's famous *Arithmetick* was published, the first treatise in English on the commercial application of 'the incomparable art' of mathematics. In it, the author insists on the importance of 'a Book to write in, or a sheet of paper to write on… ruled with lines with a black-lead Pen or a pair of Compasses'. And finally, modern lined paper was born in 1770, when Londoner John Tetlow was granted a patent for a 'machine for ruling paper for music and other purposes'.

Leaving aside paper printed for writing musical notation, there are still many different types of line, some suited

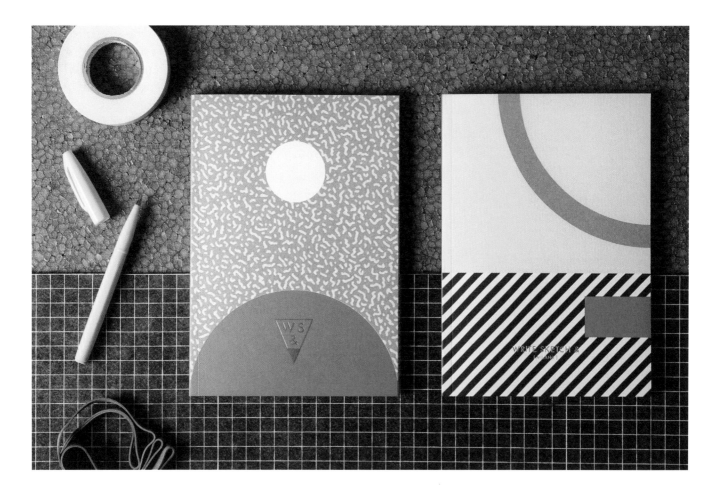

WRITE SKETCH &
Write Sketch & is a Milan-based notebook brand that embraces a funky, playful aesthetic combining the best of '80s design with top notch Italian production values. Every detail on their notebooks bespeaks quality, innovation and fun, making them a big hit with designers and creatives in Italy and beyond

to different styles of handwriting (larger or smaller), or different ends (Pitman ruling, for example, was designed with stenographers in mind).

Now, according to the almost universal ISO 216 system of paper sizes, each size of sheet of paper is equivalent to the next biggest, halved parallel to its shortest side. In other words, an A0 sheet of paper has a surface area of $1m^2$, an A1 of $50cm^2$, an A2 of $25cm^2$, and so on.

Most of the world uses the metric system, and thus the ISO 216, because it's just better. Myanmar, Liberia and the United States of America, however, do not, and as a result of this quirk in the US the geometrically elegant ISO 216 range is supplanted by a series of paper sizes derived from the pre-industrial age (precisely, from the size of the instruments used by Dutch paper craftsmen in the 1600s). One of these sizes is known as 'legal', with a legal-size sheet of paper measuring 8.5 by 14 inches.

And this is why one of the most iconic notebooks in the world is known as a 'legal notepad'. This yellow notepad, ubiquitous

NOTEBOOK WITH STENCILS
The idea behind this notebook is to allow web designers to sketch their ideas by hand before turning them into digital designs. It features a wide array of stencils, utensils, and pre-printed sketchpads, as well as a layout and a dot-grid

BARON FIG
The designs for Baron Fig were 'crowdsourced' by asking hundreds of sketchbook and notebook users for their ideas. The result is a simple but sophisticated notebook that opens flat and contains smooth paper, perfect for fountain pens

in the US, was invented in 1884 by a certain Thomas Holley, a Massachusetts paper mill worker, when he bound together some scraps of wastepaper to make a booklet for note-taking. The success of his invention led him to set up the American Pad & Paper Company (AMPAD), and it seems that the legal pad as we know it today came about when a judge asked him to manufacture a notepad with pre-ruled lines.

Having established the success of the legal pad, Thomas Holley was busted issuing fraudulent stock certificates and fled to Canada. But his invention had caught on and remains the USA's most popular notepad. In an interview with *NPR*, leading authority on the legal pad Suzanne Snider explains her take on its enduring appeal: 'it's just a beautiful object. It's already perfect. It's like the No. 2 pencil. It's a classic.' In an article for *Legal Affairs* magazine, Snider mentions just a few people who share her opinion, among them Jeff Tweedy, frontman of Wilco, and the novelist Elmore Leonard, as well as one slightly more questionable fan: '"End career as a fighter," President Richard Nixon wrote on a legal pad in August 1974.'

What, though, is the difference between a notebook and a notepad? As one dictionary somewhat tautologically puts it, a notebook is 'a small book with blank or ruled pages for writing notes in', while a notepad is 'a pad of blank or ruled pages for writing notes on'. To this we might add that a notebook's principal function is to hold pages together in one place for future reference, while a notepad is generally seen as more of a dispenser of individual sheets, which are torn out as the occasion demands. This is the reason that notebooks tend to be bound along the left hand side, as a book is, while notepads tend to be bound along the top, generally less securely, typically with some sort of gum or adhesive.

Inhabitants of Tasmania, Australia, are known informally as Taswegians, and one of their major sources of pride is that it was a Taswegian who first invented the notepad. In 1902, J. A. Birchall, owner of the stationer's in Launceston, Tasmania, started selling the Silvercity Writing Tablet, the world's first notepad (it seems that Holley's legal pad was still being bound, book-style, at this point). Until Birchall's moment, paper had always come either in notebooks or in loose sheets. His idea was to cut the sheets in half, back them with cardboard, and glue them along the top, creating a portable and orderly supply of sheets of paper.

But Birchall was standing on the shoulders of giants, and centuries of experiments in notebook binding lay behind his

STORAGE.IT
Japanese-made STORAGE.it is designed for outdoor use, incorporating a zipped bag with a clear front through which the notebook can be seen. Other items may be stored in the bag, and the cover design thus personalized

LEUCHTTURM 1917
Founded in 1917, Leuchtturm (meaning 'lighthouse' in German) sell a wide range of high quality stationery products. The journals have a table of contents and numbered pages, as well as an envelope pocket, acid-free paper and a ribbon book mark

discovery. The Italian word for notebook, 'quaderno' gives a clue as to the origin of its binding — it comes from the Latin 'quaterni', which means, roughly, 'four by four', a reference to the fact that notebooks were originally made up of groups of four sheets of paper, folded in two and bound one inside the other, giving rise to an eight-page booklet or section of a larger book. Over time more sheets were added and different techniques tried out. An example: one feature of books published before the early Twentieth Century was that their pages needed to be cut open — this was due to the fact that the printing of each eight-page section was done on a much larger piece of paper, that was then folded over on itself several times. This is why the pages of antique books often have ragged edges.

Notebooks today can be bound in a number of different ways. Sewn or hard-bound notebooks are the classic type, featuring a sewn spine like that of a printed book, from which it is hard to tear out a sheet cleanly; depending on the nature of the binding, pages will fall open flat, or drape (that is, curve). Spiral binding, by contrast, is designed precisely to facilitate the removal of sheets, featuring a coil of wire that loops through perforations along one side of the page — tearing out a

OCTAEVO
Designed and produced in Barcelona, the Octaevo range of bright colours and patterns are inspired by the Mediterranean and life by the sea. They are accompanied by a series of other products that complement the tone and feel of the notebooks

page creates that familiar umbilical cord of paper that hangs from one corner (spiral binding made its first appearance in the October, 1934 edition of *Popular Science*, FYI).

As you will have read in the little booklet that accompanies any one of the 500 paper products in the range, the Moleskine notebook is 'the heir and successor to the legendary notebook used by artists and thinkers over the past two centuries,' among them van Gogh, Picasso, Hemingway and Chatwin.

The story has been told countless times. The format in which the Moleskine is currently sold is indeed an echo of a type of small, black notebook that was made and sold in France, mainly in the early Twentieth Century. It was Bruce Chatwin who first called them 'moleskines' (a reference to the covers, made of cotton coated in linseed oil) when he sung the praises of the 'carnets moleskine' that he used to buy from a stationer's on the Rue de l'Ancienne Comédie, Paris. 'The pages were squared', Chatwin wrote in *The Songlines*, 'and the end-

TSUBAME NOTEBOOK
First produced in 1947, these hand-stitched notebooks use a special paper called 'fools paper' that is designed to work best with fountain pen. The lines are drawn using a special watercolour-based technique

TAB NOTEBOOK
This is a set of four notebooks which, as the name suggests, feature protruding tabs that help owners to organize their notebooks and keep track of their content. The ideal tool for multitaskers, designed by Moko Sellars for Suck UK

papers held in place with an elastic band.' In 1986, when he went to pick some up to take with him on a trip, Chatwin was told by the stationer that '[L]e vrai Moleskine n'est plus' — the last manufacturer of the notebooks had gone out of business.

A decade later, Maria Sebregondi read *The Songlines* and decided to trademark the Moleskine name. She pitched the concept to Italian company Modo & Modo, who duly began producing and selling the new incarnation of the notebook, this time with a synthetic binding. In 2006 Modo & Modo was bought up by a private equity firm, and in 2013 Moleskine went public — its profits in 2014 were in the region of $104 million. Moleskine now has its own chain of shops, as well as products produced in collaboration with Lego, Hello Kitty and the Simpsons. In 2012 the company moved into the digital market, partnering with Evernote to produce a notebook that syncs with smartphones.

The Moleskine notebook remains its flagship product, however. And there is no doubt that when it hit the notebook market in 1997, the Moleskine stood out both for its elegance and the quality of the materials. The company is proud of the high standard of materials used, and the sustainability of its processes (all the paper is acid-free, for example). It is also a very smooth and agreeable surface to write or draw on. The different variations on the theme cater precisely to a range of needs, from notetaking to sketching to homebrewing beer.

'To lose a passport was the least of one's worries,' Chatwin wrote, while 'to lose a notebook was a catastrophe.' And in an interview following his death,. his wife Elizabeth recalled that 'everything went into the notebooks'. There in no doubt, then, that the Moleskine was the most essential tool in Bruce Chatwin's creative process. The contents of his archive at the Bodleian library show that, apart from drafts of all his books, his moleskines contained everything from shopping lists to Sanskrit exercises, impressions of journeys to the record of a lunch with Noel Coward.

But was the moleskine format itself essential? In other words, will splashing out on a Moleskine enable you to channel Chatwin's creativity? Of course not. But as the company correctly gambled, the strong association with a mythic stationery object makes a lot of people feel that they can. And the truth is, as long as your desire is only to stamp your will on a blank piece of paper, to bring forth one of the infinite possibilities hinted at by an empty page, you are closer to Chatwin than you might think.

MOLESKINE

an interview with Maria Sebregondi

Could you tell us something most people don't know about the early days of Moleskine?

It wasn't easy to get to the first print run of 3,000 Moleskine notebooks! An infinite number of details had to be attended to before we achieved the perfection of the final object: from the bookmark and the grey tone of the lines, to the spacing of the lines themselves, the specific ivory tone of the paper — the weight and moisture content of which had to produce a particularly pleasant sound — the colour, thickness and tension of the twist stitching, and the characteristics of the elastic that holds it closed... the list could go on for hours.

But aside from the technical and aesthetic characteristics, the real leap was to look at this subject from a new point of view: not a notebook, but a book yet to be written, the book you write yourself, inspired by a great tradition. These white pages contain the essence of an important story: they trace the creative paths of great writers and artists of the past. The coloured band is designed to strengthen the idea of a book yet to be written: it evokes the band that encircles a recently-released book, that strip of paper that proclaims it the winner of a prize or carries a quotation from a famous critic. And it was as a book — albeit one still to be written — that the notebook was first sold in bookshops rather than in stationery stores, which at the time (the 1990s), especially in Italy, predominantly sold unbranded commodities. In the bookshop it found its target public in its greatest concentration, searching for information or inspiration.

What are some of the more unusual uses that you have seen a Moleskine put to?

There is a big scene around 'hacking' Moleskine objects. Also interesting is the use of custom notebooks as wedding favours, an original and striking way to make an event memorable.

To what extent do you think Moleskine has spearheaded the recent explosion of interest in stationery?

I think Moleskine has made an important contribution to this growing passion: the Moleskine notebook is indeed an archetype of the paper base necessary for any expression of writing or drawing. Its aesthetic, functional and symbolic characteristics constitute a solid base on which to build a passion that extends to all analogue cognitive artefacts.

What future do you think stationery objects have in an ever-more digitalized world?

I think this passion is destined to last for a long time. As human beings we are deeply connected to physical gestuality, the aesthetics of the objects that we use for the most eminently human activities: to discover, to learn, to express ourselves, to create... Technology tends to absorb the functional elements of these activities to make them simpler and faster, but it struggles to enhance the aesthetic and symbolic aspects (and when it does, it is extraordinarily successful, as in the case of Apple). Of course, we're talking about niches and not the mass market — but niches are interesting, even in terms of numbers!

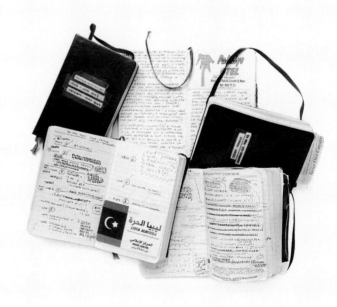

FABER

German Paper
QUALITY STANDARD

FABER

```
┌─────────────────────────────────┐
│                                 │
│            FABER                │
│                                 │
├─────────────────────────────────┤
│            PRODUCER             │
├────────────────┬────────────────┤
│     Osaka      │     Japan      │
└────────────────┴────────────────┘
```

Homo Faber Fortunae Suae: man is the craftsman of his own destiny. This is the idea that inspires the Faber: Notebooks for Practice collection. Designed in Italy by creator Longa and produced in Japan, Faber embodies an approach to design that brings together the handmade and the mass-produced, giving rise to limited-edition notebooks that cry out to be looked at, handled, treasured.

"The first Faber notebooks were designed at the end of 2014 and developed during the spring of 2015, and the public launch of the online store was in September 2015. As an illustrator and graphic designer, I had always been interested in paper. When I was a child, I would watch my aunt (who worked as a bookbinder in her youth) binding my comics with my mother. I started producing and selling handmade notebooks about 8 years ago, when I was living in Italy. With an interest bookbinding and stationery in general, I've always tried to create notebooks with a design approach, far removed from the stereotypes of 'craft' and 'DIY' styles. I just wanted to create something I couldn't find in stores.

Once the business had started to grow a little I soon realized why that kind of product was not on the shelves: the production steps, materials and details were too laborious

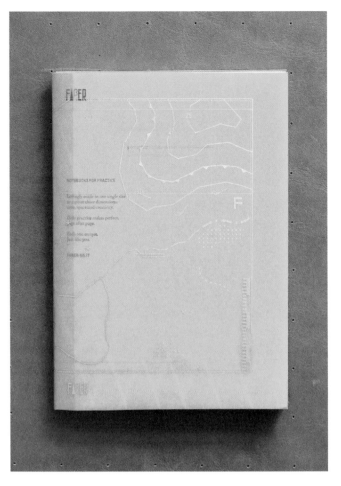
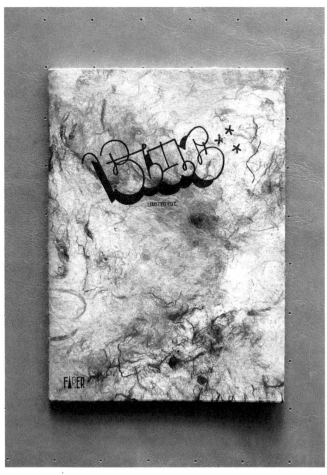

All Faber notebooks deploy a
tangibly hand-made aesthetic

and expensive to be reproduced in a mechanical and
more industrialized way. So I gave up making handmade
notebooks and developed a limited edition of 12 designs,
once a month for a year, exploring this tension between
production and handmade manufacture. My goal was to
create a product with the 'right' tension between industrial
and handmade production, on both the design and the
production side. Moving to Japan in 2014 was the spark that
started the Faber Project.

The people who buy my notebooks tend to be stationery lovers
and maniacs for details, as well as people who are interested
in 'the story' of what they have in their hands. I also love it
when store staff explain what is behind a certain product. I
feel that good products demand a mutual education between
the designer (who develops the project) and the customer (who
buys the result).

For my project, stationery is limited to the desk. In truth,
I'm not interested in creating a lifestyle brand. I like to

concentrate on a specific path and follow it, and I don't feel this is a limitation. I draw a lot of inspiration from design in general, from product design to architecture. I'm fascinated by old stuff, not necessarily fancy or exotic items. I'm very fond of common stationery items with the allure of nostalgia.

At the moment, the 'Tic Toc - Time is the Monster' notebook is highly appreciated by my clients. The first release of notebooks is based on the same structure for the three styles, so I personally love all the styles, although my favourite is probably the Creativity one, the simplest of the three. I love the waxed paper used in the cover-jacket.

In terms of stationery, I love mechanical pencils from Rotring and the vintage Pentel ones, Seed and vintage Koh-i-noor erasers, scissors from Tajika and Takeji Hasami, and table complements by 22studio and Plan-S23, to name only a few. When it comes to notebooks, I truly love the basic Kokuyo PRO line and Hum notebooks."

CAD ERNO SORT IDO

PUBLICAÇÕES SERROTE

PRODUCER, LETTERPRESS	
Lisbon	Portugal

Serrote makes beautiful, beautiful notebooks. Founded in 2004 by Susana Vilela and Nuno Neves, Serrote products are designed using antique letterpress type and ornaments, creating an aesthetic that melds the traditional and hyper-contemporary. Drawing on everything from the Lisbon sky to traditional Portuguese visual culture, their limited-edition runs of notebooks entrance the eye and mind.

"We started our project towards the end of 2004, with the goal of producing a notebook with a cover printed in letterpress. Having studied Fine Art and Design, we were familiar with the technology, but we had never got the opportunity to work with it. Looking for traditional print shops in Lisbon, we realized many of them were closing down. After a good deal of searching we found a traditional letterpress shop, tucked away in an old neighbourhood, where typesetters were still printing invoices and business cards the old way. We searched in old cases for metal type and produced the first project: a notebook with the cover printed in two colours in letterpress, and with a blue plain book block, printed in a limited edition of 500.

At the time we thought that if we weren't able to sell them then at least we would have notebooks for the rest of our lives.

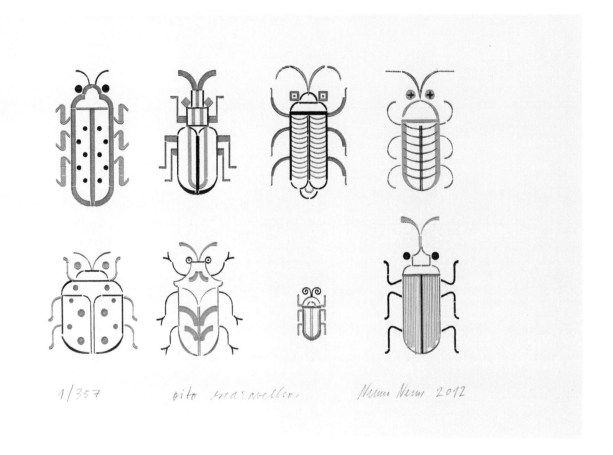

1/357   oito maravilhas   Nuno Neves 2012

Some insects composed by using
letterpress shapes

Opposite page, below: how the
compositions are made

But we set up a website for our brand and one and only product, and got some positive feedback from a number of stores in Portugal, as well as articles in a few newspapers and blogs. Given the positive results, we produced soon after a squared notebook, and we went on increasing the notebook collection. In the meantime, most of the old traditional printer shops closed down, but as we to acquired old metal type, ornaments and presses, nowadays we can print our projects by ourselves.

Our core project is to explore the potential and technical limitations of letterpress; we make new compositions reusing old type and ornaments that used to be used to print receipts, business cards, and packaging, placing them in new contexts. We also like to create different notebooks, beyond the traditional plain, squared or ruled, with new patterns and textures, which gives the user a new perspective and experience of handwriting or drawing. Our letterpress projects are printed in limited and numbered series.

We started our project with a collection of notebooks of the same size and with the same number of pages, but our catalogue has grown in multiple directions. It now includes more notebooks

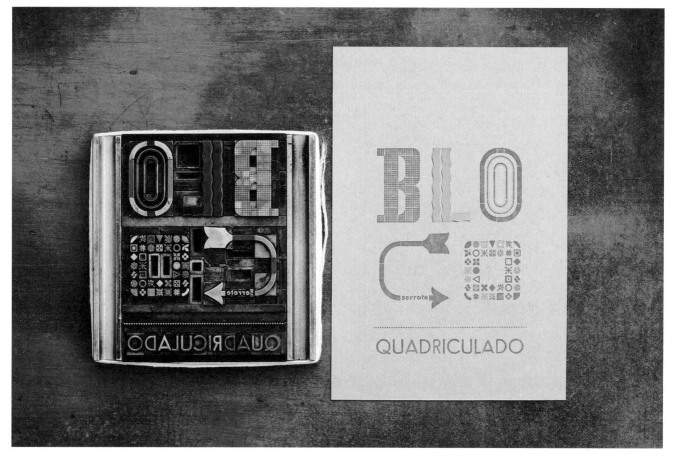

(with different sizes and papers) notepads, diaries and card sets. And we make also prints, illustrated books, posters, and have produced a wooden crate filled with 10 products specially made in collaboration with other Portuguese manufacturers.

Our most popular product is the 'Caderno Toalha de Mesa' (tablecloth notebook), filled with the traditional textured tablecloth paper used at the tables of Portuguese restaurants, and usually scribbled on after meals. Every project has a special place in our hearts. Some were tougher to make, some are prettier than others, some are smarter and some sell better than others. However Susana is very fond of the 'Caderno Sabão Azul & Branco', based on traditional blue and white marbled soaps, with the cover printed in letterpress and the pages of the inside filled with these soap patterns. Nuno prefers Bloco Celeste, a notepad with 144 plain pages of four different tones interleaved with each other, producing a gradient from blue to white; it reproduces the colours of a daytime sky. We are inspired by our trips around Portugal, and specially by the 'anonymous design' found in the old business cards, packaging, traffic and store signs, etc.

And there are two shops that we love, where everything is worth discovering, trying or buying: Present & Correct, a British shop, focused on stationery and vintage office supplies from over the world; and A Vida Portuguesa, a Portuguese shop focused on Portuguese manufacture, from soaps to pencils, from cookies to textiles."

On these pages, a selection of Serrote letterpress notebooks

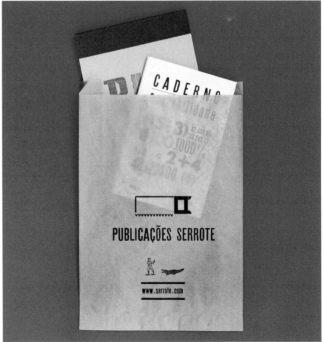

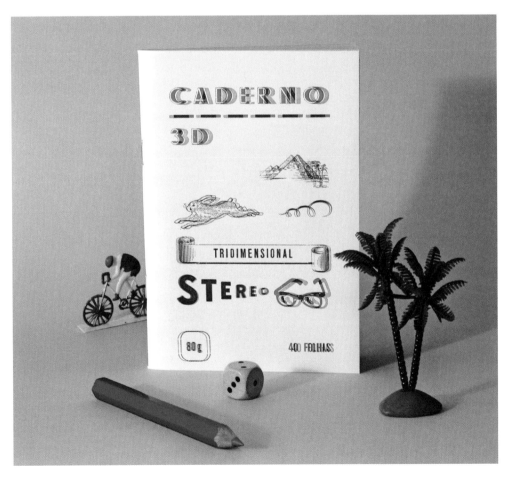

Founded in 2010 by graphic designer Kateřina Šachová, Papelote aims to re-establish the forgotten beauty of paper, considering it as 'a material full of flavour, fragrance, sound and colour'. With its bricks-and-mortar store in Prague, Papelote sells a range of notebooks, sketchbooks and related products, all of them made in the Czech Republic from environmentally-friendly materials. There is also a Papelote creative studio, which designs and produces bespoke stationery for clients.

"Our motto is 'the body and soul of paper'. Paper means more to us than a simple base for writing: it is a material full of flavour, fragrance, sound, and colour. Our main goals are to bring a fresh breeze into the world of paper, as well as offer an alternative to current paper production.

I think that a lot of people are coming back to using paper, especially because of the widespread use of digital technology, which on one hand makes our lives simpler but at the same time can overwhelm us. Paper offers a completely different experience, provoking unique feelings that no mobile application can ever substitute.

What I love about stationery is that it waits for its owner to tell the story. It lives and breathes in interaction with people.

I am always very happy to see that our customers are far from a homogenous group, from children and young students, women and men, to older people. What I love is the diversity. It reinforces my vision of paper as an intergenerational connector. Digital media — especially the web and social networks — are very important for us. Indeed, I think they've become indispensable. They should not replace human contact, though: that is essential for us — the physical presence more than the virtual one.

Papelote currently offers a wide range of products, from pencils, notebooks, diaries, journals, photo albums, letter sets, or wrapping paper, to various folders and simple cases. The limits are set mainly by our current capacity. I imagine that those limits will eventually stretch even further, to include school bags or desks.

My decisions about what to sell are intuitive; I feel, when something is missing, that something needs to be changed, added, abandoned (as it is with life). Our most popular items vary, and their popularity comes in waves.

A selection of Papelote products, distinguished by their brights, playful colour scheme

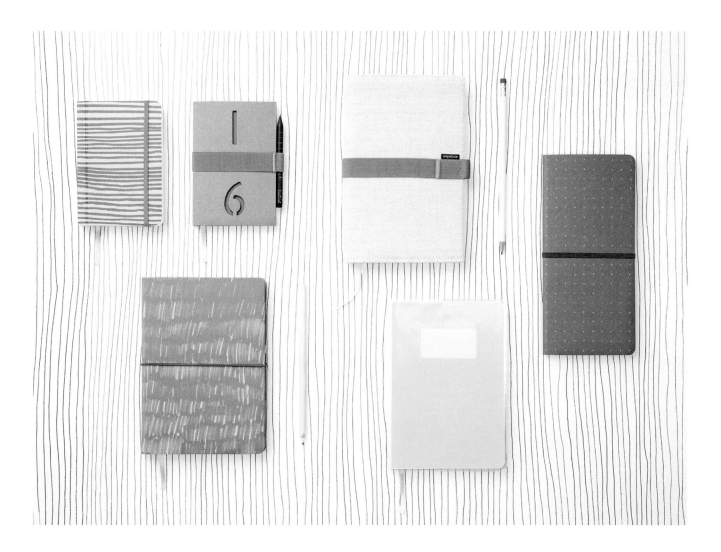

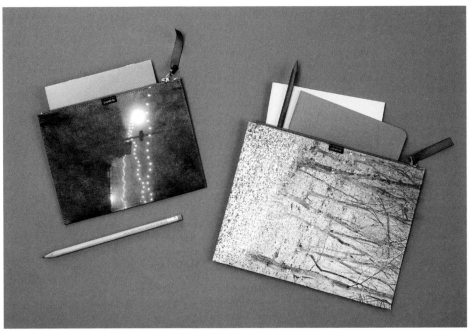

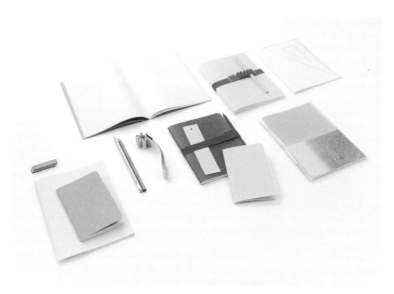

A further selection of Papelote products

Opposite: interior of the shop, featur-ing an innovative system of clips to display products

Our Spiral notepads with a notebook strap for five pens or pencils have always been very popular, probably because they are simple and practical. Our Professio notebooks, which have a colour-stitched binding, also sell very well. Most recently, our new photo albums have become very popular.

One of my favourite products has from the very beginning been the Envelopa notebook, the cover of which is made from a folded envelope, which creates a practical pocket to store all sorts of scraps of paper or loose notes. It fulfils my idea of harmonizing simplicity with invention.

I think that stationery's current resurgence is due, most of all, to a lack of tactility in the contemporary world. People miss it. Touch is one of the most important senses — maybe the most important. One touch can say more than a handful of words. Paper is an ingenious invention. We can touch it, smell it, or tear it apart and burn it in anger. Or, on the contrary, we can keep it and, after many years, we can be reminded of something that may be long gone. Paper can preserve our feelings, memories, thoughts, and wishes, not only for ourselves but, perhaps, for our children, grandchildren and friends. This way it becomes our personal memory bank, and I think that's what people are passionate about."

CHAPTER Nº6

GLUE

———

Love will stick us together

Sticking things to other things: there's more to it than you might think. A lot more, in fact, as Floyd L. Darrow's seminal *The Story of an Ancient Art: From the Earliest Adhesives to Vegetable Glue* (1930) makes clear. 'What is there of beauty in the unsightly glue pot?' asks Darrow. 'Are there any great names among the devotees of the time-honoured practice of applying an adhesive to make a perfect joint?' The answer is yes, and foremost among them is that of Dr Wolfgang Dierichs, creator of the world's most iconic adhesive, the Pritt Stick.

Top: period Pritt advertising

Dr Dierichs was a researcher in the adhesives area of the German company Henkel. Founded in 1876, Henkel came to prominence with Persil, the first 'self-activated' laundry detergent. They got into glue when French and Belgian troops occupied the Rhineland in 1924 and made it impossible for them to obtain the glue they needed for the Persil packaging. The company is today the world's biggest producer of adhesives.

A large part of this success is unquestionably a result of the moment in 1967 when the young Dr Dierichs watched a woman put on her lipstick, and realized that the twisty applicator could work equally well with adhesives. Dierichs' brainstorm was to banish 'the unsightly gluepot' from classrooms and offices forever. Since then, more than a billion Pritt Sticks, as his invention was named, have been sold in 121 countries. The Pritt has been so successful and useful an object that (as often happens in the world of stationery) in some countries this one brand name has come to be used interchangeably with the object itself, despite the proliferation of inferior alternatives that followed its first release.

One of the Pritt Stick's major rivals in the glue sphere is the flagship product of another German company. Invented in 1932 by a chemist called Fischer, UHU was the world's first clear synthetic resin adhesive. Its utility guaranteed it widespread success, and Fischer's glue was used on the interior of the Hindenburg Zeppelin, among other places.

UHU's name comes from the onomatopoeic German word for the eagle owl: in German it is pronounced oo-hoo, whereas in English it is you-hoo, hence the marketing slogan, 'Don't say glue, say UHU'. In Germany they use the legend 'Der Alleskleber', which means 'the all-sticker', a much less catchy catchphrase which nonetheless seems to have worked as, like Pritt in the UK, UHU in Germany has become a synonym (or genericized trademark) for glue.

But there are other types of adhesive, of course. 'Sellotape' is the brand name by which adhesive tape is known in many countries, among them the UK. In fact, the substance known as adhesive or pressure-sensitive tape is, like glue, generally referred by brand names — in the US it is universally called Scotch.

The science behind Sellotape/Scotch is fearfully clever, and far beyond the remit of this book. In the words of Dr Spencer Silver, inventor of the Post-it, adhesives 'are very different to glue... Glue is a very simplistic term. You boil animal bones down and make something that sticks when it dries. Adhesives are completely different. They rely on a complex structure of molecules to create their tack and elasticity.'

Some period advertising for UHU, 'the all-sticker'

Above: a selection of different kind of vintage tape

In short, the characteristic that unites all types of tape, from duct to hockey, is that they consist of a pressure-sensitive adhesive, applied to a strip of material. The first model was designed in 1845 by a surgeon by the name of Dr Horace Day, who invented a kind of surgical tape by applying a rubber adhesive to strips of cloth. The next step forward in tape technology arose from the needs of the automobile industry, which had come to require a tape that would enable them to achieve a neat finish when spray-painting cars. In 1925, the Minnesota Mining and Manufacturing Company (today better known by the name of 3M, the world's biggest tape manufacturer) came up with masking tape, in a format not too different to how it looks today.

3M also pioneered the tape dispenser. As everyone who has ever used a pressure-sensitive adhesive tape, to give it its full name, knows, the trickiest part of the whole operation is finding the end of the roll. 3M recognized, and solved, this problem almost as soon as they had invented the stuff, in 1932 releasing a dispenser with a built-in blade, to which the end of the tape stuck. But the creative titan of the dispenser world was the industrial designer Jean Otis Reinecke. Reinecke's second design for 3M was a heavy, cast-metal tape dispenser in grey, which he updated in 1953. But his masterpiece was the Decor Dispenser Model C-15, that was launched by 3M in 1961 and continued to be sold until the end of the century.

Available in a range of colours, the Decor Dispenser Model C-15 is a desktop classic, notwithstanding the fact that one of the models turned out to be slightly radioactive, due to the fact that

Then there's Blu-tack, another genericized adhesive product (although in Finland it's known as 'Kennaratyggjó', meaning 'teacher's chewing gum'). Blu-tack was in fact invented by a researcher at a sealant factory, who came up with a semi-elastic putty-like substance that didn't seal anything, but could be used to stick paper to walls. The original makers weren't interested in it and gave the idea to Bostik, who eventually developed the product as we know it today. Originally white, it was given a blue colour in response to fears that children would mistake it for gum

monazite sand, which contains thorium, was used as ballast. Reinecke was also responsible for designing the disposable plastic Scotch tape dispenser, a classic of cheap but impeccably functional design. In fact, tape dispensers are a fascinating subgenre of deskware, blurring as they do the line between form and function; it is well worth scanning the offerings on eBay.

3M's most recognizable innovation in the field of adhesion is so widespread as to be almost invisible. Like shoes or the internet, it is hard to fathom that there was a time when the Post-it note didn't exist, and harder still to think that at some point someone said 'fiat Post-it', and invented them. But someone did: a Dr Spencer Silver, to be precise, a scientist at 3M who in 1968 stumbled across a reusable pressure-sensitive adhesive. Calling it a 'solution without a problem', Dr Silver spent five years trying to promote his discovery, but to no avail. Then in 1974 a colleague of his hit on the rather quaint solution of using the adhesive to hold his bookmark in his hymnbook. 3M ran with the idea, eventually coming up with Press 'n Peel sticky note, launched in 1977. The product was relaunched in 1980 as Post-it notes and shot to success.

The Post-it is very emblematic of stationery in general. While they represented the culmination of decades of technical and scientific progress, and revolutionized how offices work (in these days of 'track changes', it is easy to underestimate the impact that Post-its had), they are so ubiquitous that is it easy to overlook them, and surely few people ever idly wondered who their inventor was. Like oxygen, stationery is all around us, but we only really notice it when it runs out.

COCCOINA

Coccoina represents a pocket of resistance to the world domination of Pritt Stick and UHU. Manufactured in 1927 by the Balma, Capoduri & C., it was the first glue to be manufactured in Italy, and its solvent-free composition has remained all but unchanged: generation on generation of Italians experience a nostalgic kick whenever they scent its characteristic, almondy fragrance. Refreshingly, everything from the distinctive packaging to the brushes are still made internally at Balma, Capoduri. & C.

The coccoina packaging, unchanged since the company was founded

Some period advertising

MT MASKING TAPE

PRODUCER, TAPE	
Kurashiki	Japan

'Washi washi' is a colourful, reusable, semi-transparent, quintessentially Japanese masking tape. The MT brand is a product of the Kamoi Kakoshi company, which has for the last 100 years been a leading producer of specialty paper adhesives in Japan. (Washi itself is an ancient Japanese handmade paper).

In 2006, Kamoi Kakoshi launched this range of colourful masking tape explicitly for creative uses. It is easy to tear by hand, and can be stuck on almost any surface and repositioned. It comes in hundreds of semi-transparent colours that can be combined to make new patterns and colour tones. It is also easy to write on.

Made of natural fibres, Washi tape is a massive internet phenomenon. Its versatility makes it ideal for creative decorating. As it is easy to apply and then remove, it can be used to prepare spaces for parties or celebrations.

MT washi washi masking tape features patterns or geometric shapes, or a range of different designs. It is also available in a series of extremely funky finishes (the 'Fab' line). Kamoi Kakoshi have produced a series of models in collaboration with different designers and artists from all over the world.

Previous spread and opposite
page: some colourful examples
of MT washi tape

Right: the production process

Below: MT tape in action

CHAPTER Nº 7

POST

Pushing
the envelope

Coleridge called Theodore Hook 'as true a genius as Dante'. It is both ironic and apt that, rather than for the fifty-odd volumes of his collected writings, Hook is today remembered only as the inventor of that most ephemeral of art forms, the postcard. The British postal service was modernized in 1840, and in that same year Hook sent himself a hand-drawn cartoon, simply by affixing one of the new Penny Black stamps to the back, alongside his Fulham address. The world's first adhesive postage stamp, the Penny Black is now incredibly rare, and it is no surprise that Hook's ground-breaking postal innovation fetched over thirty thousand pounds when it was auctioned in 2002.

Deltiology is the name given to the study of the rich and fascinating history of postcards, which deltiologists break down into various epochs, starting with the Golden Age (1898–1919). The first printed postcard we know about dates from 1870, but it wasn't until the late Nineteenth Century that the industry really started booming, thanks largely to the expansion of rail travel that enabled the masses to go on holiday to the seaside. The Eiffel Tower, too, contributed, generating a massive souvenir industry which it sustains to this day. The French were also the initiators of a sub-genre known as 'French postcards', featuring what to modern eyes may seem fairly chaste photographs of young ladies in the nude, sold under the counter in insalubrious stationers the world over (in the USA this term remained current for a long time — witness the first scene of the Coen Brothers' *Hail Caesar*).

There seems to have been something about the postcard format that encouraged the lubricious. Donald McGill, Britain's most famous postcard artist, was so prolific that many people no doubt think his oeuvre constituted a whole school or style, rather than the fruit of but one man's cheerfully sexist

"Four nice marrows you have there, Mrs. Ramsbottom!"

Above: a cheeky McGill postcard

imagination; as George Orwell asked in his 1941 essay on him: 'Who does not know the 'comics' of the cheap stationers' windows, the penny or twopenny coloured post cards with their endless succession of fat women in tight bathing-dresses and their crude drawing and unbearable colours?'

Over the course of his career McGill created an estimated 12,000 saucy postcard designs, and over 200 million copies of them were sold. Their subjects tended towards a very mid-century British sense of humour, also much in evidence in the *Carry On* movies, heavy on vicars and bosoms and only-just-double entendre. 'She's a nice girl,' one gentleman comments to his companion, both of them eyeing the buxom lady in the foreground of one postcard: 'Doesn't drink or smoke, and only swears when it slips out.' 'Do you like Kipling?' a young man asks a woman in another, holding up a copy of Kim. 'I don't know, you naughty boy,' comes the reply, 'I've never kippled.' (This one sold six million copies.)

Although unamused, Orwell saw these postcards as 'a sort of saturnalia, a harmless rebellion against virtue'. In the USA

HAND STAMPS

———

A hand stamp generally features an image or design on a rubber sheet attached to a handle, often made of wood. These are used to stamp ink impressions wherever such impressions are needed. Hand stamps fall into one of three categories. The first is the classic model, which requires a little pad with a sponge soaked in ink, a favourite of librarians and passport officials.

The second type are self-inking, which contain an inbuilt ink supply: upon pressing down on them, the die flips round 180 degrees to make its impression. The third type is pre-inked, in which the die itself is impregnated with ink, like those ones teachers use at school to put happy or sad or simply indifferent faces at the bottom of your work.

this period in postcard history is comparatively staid and decorative. Known in deltiology as the linen postcard era, 1931 to circa-1950 was a period in which a cheap card stock with a high rag content was used to print postcards, which were then finished in a linen-like texture, possibly to suggest the appearance of a canvas.

Linen postcards typically featured landscapes, urban ones above all, some distinctly redolent of Edward Hopper, as well as brash typographical experiments. Their rich, bright colours captivated generations of holidaymakers, and even though Kodachrome was first piloted in 1936, it took a decade and a half for what is known as the Chrome era of postcard-making to kick in. These glossy-finish, realistically coloured photographs continue to define what we mean by a postcard.

And then there is the postage stamp. We saw that the first stamp ever made was the Penny Black. Prior to its invention, letters were franked using hand stamps (which is where

LETTER OPENER

―――――――

The letter opener or paper knife is an object more or less similar to a knife that is typically used to open letters, although Martin Luther King is one of several people known to have been stabbed by one, in his case not fatally. Letter openers tend to be long and slim and, while they are often made of metal, their sharpness is not paramount, which is why you can find examples made of ivory or Bakelite, for example.

The origin of the letter opener is the paper knife, an essential reader's tool in the days before the mechanization of book production. The way that books were put together meant that in many cases every page had to be cut open along its outermost edge, much in the manner that letters are sliced open today. A pen knife with its stubby, over-sharp blade was inadequate to this task, as it tended to rip the pages, or at best leave an uneven, ragged edge. The paper knife by contrast applies a steady pressure across most of the page.

The smoothness of the paper knife was also crucial in guaranteeing a clean edge, and the best were made of ivory, mother of pearl, or hardwoods like mahogany. Probably the most well-known paper knife in literature is in Jean Paul Sartre's play *No Exit*, in which three people are trapped together in a room in hell. At the climax, one of them picks up a paper knife and stabs another with it, only for her intended victim to remind her that she is already dead.

More of the beautiful and unique cards
and postcards on sale at R.S.V.P. Berlin

the name comes from) and ink, and post was paid for by the recipient, on delivery. This gave rise to the obvious problem that the postal service could not recuperate the cost of delivery if the recipient couldn't be found or didn't want to pay, and the pre-1840 service was a shambles. The pre-paid postage stamp constituted an elegant and effective solution to the problem, and even from day one generated an interest that went beyond the merely functional: the zoologist Dr. John Gray bought several Penny Blacks when they were released with the intention simply of preserving them, making him the world's first stamp collector.

The world of stamps is vast and endlessly absorbing. For a century and half, most countries in the world churned out mini-masterpiece after mini-masterpiece, generating an industry and an enthusiasm unique in the history of collecting. But the stamp would of course be functionally useless without the envelope to which it is affixed — although the stamp is the star of the show, without the blank canvas of the envelope, it would be no more than a pretty face. Likewise, a letter is just a sheet of paper with writing

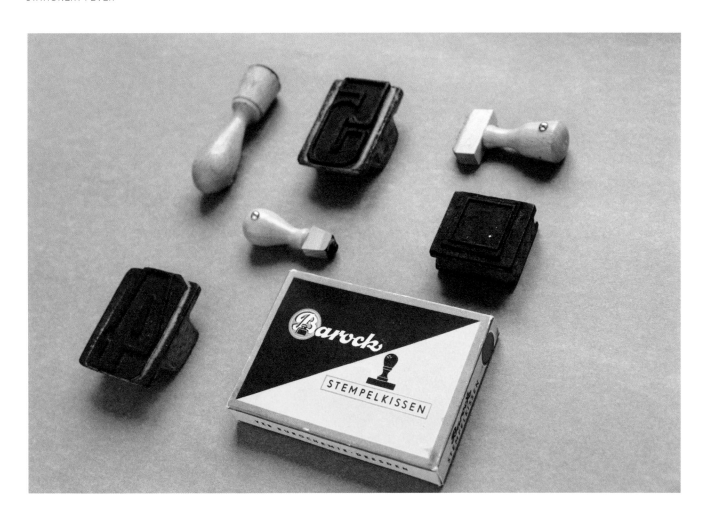

Some handstamps and a 'Barock' ink pad produced between 1950-1970. A gorgeous example of classic GDR (German Democratic Republic) stationery design

on, until it is slid inside the envelope. In short, without the mediation of the unassuming envelope, the whole concept of post just breaks down, so it is to this often overlooked stationery item that we must now turn.

Always ahead of the game when it came to paper, it was the Chinese who first developed the envelope, using them to distribute money. In Europe it was not until the explosion set off by the appearance of the first stamp that paper envelopes appeared on the scene, when in 1845 Edwin Hill and Warren De La Rue were granted a patent for a stream-driven envelope-making machine. The envelopes they produced were creased and folded, but it was up to the user to decide how to stick them. They came in a shape not dissimilar to a modern 'baronial' envelope, that enabled all four flaps to be held in place with a single wax seal (another 50 years were to pass before the invention of the pre-gummed envelope).

The window envelope, through which the address can be read, was patented in 1901, and has become a standard bit of business

Martin Z. Schröder, Letterpress printed card

stationery. Various other shapes, types and variants became available, but the next major shake up in the envelope world came in 1998, with the introduction in the US of the Electronic Stamp Distribution (ESD) system, which enabled envelopes to be fed into a printer and stamped directly with a digital frank, removing altogether the need for a postage stamp.

While this development produced consternation across the industry and among philatelists worldwide, the death knell had already been sounded for the envelope and the postage stamp alike. Electronic mail has little in common with real mail, but it has come to all but supplant its role in personal and professional communication. In the not quite two decades since it was popularized on a massive scale (Hotmail started in 1996, Gmail in 2004) email has come to seem an essential and inevitable feature of life, while letters, envelopes and stamps now feel quaint if not retrograde, like rolodex or spittoons. The envelope has, however, been guaranteed a weird kind of zombie afterlife in its symbolic use within email programs. How long before most of the people who click the 'send' button will have no idea why it features that little geometric ideogram?

SEALING WAX

Prior to the development of modern postal services, those few people who could and needed to send letters relied on a technique involving sealing wax. The basic process involved folding your letter over and melting some special wax (generally of a crimson colour) onto the flap, and then impressing your signet ring into it before it hardened.

The wax sealed shut the letter, making it impossible to open without snapping the seal. The mark of the signet ring in the wax was an added guarantee of authenticity, bearing your specific insignia. Sealing wax is a different type to that used in candles, and normally comes in sticks which are melted, without being burned or blackened, directly onto the paper.

BONVINI

SHOP, STATIONERY	
Milan	Italy

Bonvini is a revolutionary and dynamic project. A group of friends took over an antique stationer's and printworks in Milan and, without changing the nature of the site, expanded its activities to include a range of stationery- and design-related spaces, among them a printing press, and a typewriter repair workshop. In a short space of time, Bonvini has become an obligatory visit for any stationery lover passing through Italy. Here we talk to Edoardo Fonti, one of the founders, about the project.

"Fratelli Bonvini Milano is a historic workshop founded over a century ago: a little piece of the history of Milan. The workshop was on the point of disappearing but a group of friends have recovered, carefully restored, and returned it to the city, allowing old stories to continue and new ones to be started. We reopened the Fratelli Bonvini stationery and printing shop at the end of 2014, and in this short time it has already been populated with new adventures.

Our customers are of many different ages and backgrounds: Artists, designers, architects, young makers, lovers of writing and calligraphy, experimenters with ancient techniques mixed with new technologies and contemporary aesthetics. These different people are united by a passion for artisanal crafts related to paper, writing, drawing, stamps

Previous spread: some of the beautiful
calligraphy nibs available at Bonvini

Above: Bonvini is still working through
the archive of the original owners of
the workshop

and movable type — a world of analogue artifacts and their
different expressions.

There are a lot of things to be found at Fratelli Bonvini:
stationery, typography books, small exhibitions of artists
who work with typography and calligraphy, events,
collections of chairs, recipes and archives. We are planting
the seeds of a desire to make by hands, the uniqueness of
gestures and experiences that arise from making analog,
physical networks, with the new languages that technology
makes possible. A place to get to know old and new
equipment, the accelerator and the Imperia together with
the 3D printer. Old and new services: business cards and one-
off and serial pieces, flyers and posters.

The range of products and services available are defined
primarily by the interests, skills and passions of the
members: we are the first recipients of what is happening
here. Sensitivity, attention to detail and severe critical
acumen are interwoven with the opportunities that flourish
around us. To select in this vast territory, to curate and

The original shopfront of the Bonvini shop

edit what makes sense for us and our public, is always the most complex task: a delicate balance between the legacy of the past to be preserved, the offerings of the present, and the anticipation of the future.

Technology is wonderful, but — it's even a cliché — it is a homogenizing force, and tends to give rise to creative flattening and standardization. It speeds up and simplifies the path to realization, but the creative process runs the risk of being crushed. Particularly those working in creative professions feel more and more the need to recapture the uniqueness of the analogue gesture on paper, to keep track of progressive developments of an idea, to find a balance between the verticality of analogue making and the horizontality of digital making.

There are many individual objects that characterize the history of Bonvini. Some, like the '50s and' 60s nibs, are kept in small handmade drawers. And then there are hundreds of historic pencil models manufactured in Europe since the '30s, often in packaging that is fascinating, thanks to the graphic design and the detail of the description. However, I shall focus on the ability that a place like Bonvini has to attract forgotten and apparently lifeless stories and objects. Items arrive and are taken up by us, to discover their use and give them a proper home. So here we have the Swiss sharpener built around an replaceable razor blade, the mimeograph from the '50s, the fully functional 1973 typewriter, the packaging for storing business cards made by hand from corrugated cardboard. We are also organizing and cataloging the archive, which includes all the printing material, the characters and the printing plates, and the small printing equipment. Other discoveries remain to be made.

Being a digital native allows you to discover the beauty and the wealth of experience built into and preserved by fully analogue objects. The rapid obsolescence of technology products makes us appreciate the durability of objects that are simple but in their own way perfect, such as a pencil or a binder. We live in the knowledge economy, and what produces economic value in any field is the ability to innovate: the creative process is the key to innovation, and is based on the

Many of the period furnishings of
the shop have been left unchanged
since it was taken over

talent and the wealth of knowledge of each interaction of
people and things. Cognitive artifacts and analogue activities
that involve the senses contribute to shaking up habitual
perspectives, to changing the way in which we remember, and
they are therefore increasingly engines of ideas and creativity.

In the growing immateriality of the digital, more and more we
need concrete fragments of memory, physical evidence of the
past, yellowed photographs, postcards of disappeared places, old
letters ... Sometimes even the memories of others can help form
and consolidate mobile identities, to build elements of your
own biography through fragments of other people's stories."

TAMPOGRAPHE SARDON

SHOP, PRODUCER	
Paris	France

Two Lenins locked in a passionate kiss. An intricate, bi-colour Day of the Dead skull. Kitschy cherubs holding up a wreath encircling the words '*Tu me fais chier.*' Paris atelier Le Tampographe Sardon has breathed new life into an all-but-moribund art form, making beautiful, edgy, hilarious rubber stamps.

A few minutes walk from the tomb of Jim Morrison, Le Tampographe Sardon is on the front line of alt stationery design. Vincent Sardon, who previously worked at *Le Monde* newspaper, set up the studio seven years ago, and his designs have steadily acquired a cult following in France and beyond — he has had exhibitions in different places around Europe.

Previous spread and current pages:
a selection of playful and provocative
designs by Tampographe Sardon,
alongside an image of the studio window

Sardon's work expresses a mordantly ironic view of life, and in particular the place of the artist within it. As shown by the texts accompanying his monograph published in 2011, he is gifted with a highly literary intelligence, which works in raucous harmony with his flair for punchy, punky design.

A rather hermit-like figure, he will not let photographs of himself be published, and spends most of his time shut up in his modestly-sized studio. In the mornings, he uses the heat from his huge Italian-made industrial stamp machine to toast his breakfast panini, trying to ignore the after-taste of burnt rubber it gives them.

SCHOOL

Unpacking
the pencil case

School supplies are big money. There are few markets that have such a guaranteed, consistent and predictable flow of demand, and this is why big stationery companies jostle for classroom dominance so energetically. But more than its commercial prospects, the stationery we used at school continues to exert a strong nostalgic pull. The smell of PVC glue, for example, or the taste of a fresh Crayola are able to transport us back in time to happier, more stationery-filled days. Let's revisit some old friends.

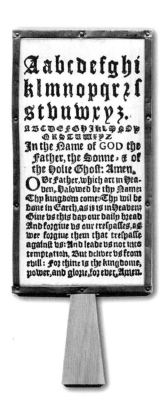

A hornbook from the Middle Ages,
used to teach children their ABC

A English battledore published
by William Davison in 1830

ARMADO (to Holofernes): Monsieur, are you not lett'red?
MOTH: Yes, he teaches boys the hornbook.

This dry little exchange from *Love's Labours Lost* will be
impenetrable, unless you know that one of the first items
of school supplies in recorded history is the hornbook, a
wooden tablet inscribed with the alphabet, used from the
1400s onwards to teach children to read. Later hornbooks
also featured a syllabarium, to help learners with vowel/
consonant combos. The battledore, a later, more sophisticated
version of the hornbook, would accompany capital letters
with an image illustrating them — an apple for 'A', a king
for 'K', and a mouse for 'M', for example — just as modern
classroom aids do.

But school supplies as we understand them today reflect
important sociological changes that came about towards
the end of the Nineteenth Century, when compulsory mass
education was instituted across Europe and in the US,
provoking a huge expansion of demand for basic classroom
products. This occurred in tandem with the early stages of
mass-production, and many items that we are going to look at
here remain icons of industrial design.

One of the main needs of these new generations of diminutive
consumers was to transport their things to and from school.
At first, children carried their books and notebooks held
together with a belt. In the early to mid-Twentieth Century
the school bag or satchel began to enjoy prominence, and
backpacks remain the receptacle of choice; a child's preference
for make and design, as well as the customizations they make,
often reflect an important process of identity formation.

Above: a 1940s Mexican notebook and bi-coloured lead holder of the same period

Below: an original pee-chee folder

Folders likewise became increasingly important as the past century progressed, in particular when photocopies came to replace the taking of notes from the blackboard. The first Pee-Chee folder (an American mid-century classic, so called for its peach colour) was produced in 1943, while the Trapper Keeper binder was launched in the '70s, becoming one of the most well-known school brands in the history of US stationery. They feature a three-ring binder and a Velcro-sealed flap, to make sure your papers don't fly out when it is hurled across the classroom.

And complementing the file or folder is, of course, the pencil case. Although custom-made boxes for transporting pens had been around for as long as pens themselves, it wasn't until 1949 that a certain Verona Pearl Amoth filed a patent in the US for a case 'wherein the holding of the pencils eliminates breaking thereof when carried in their orderly manner'.

We look at length at pens, pencils, erasers and sharpeners elsewhere in this book. But a modern pencil case has to hold

Below: vintage training compasses to learn the basic of geometry

more than just essential writing implements. An important feature, still, is the ruler and its variants. The classic plastic 30cm 'shatterproof' is the go-to school ruler; after being snapped in some non-sanctioned activity, truncated chunks of it remain serviceable. Then there is the non-essential and hence highly desirable ruler that has a sort of cylinder built in to it, to facilitate the ruling of parallel lines. And there was a time when, upon attaining a certain age, children were expected to buy a special geometry set containing a protractor (the plastic half-circle), set squares (the pair of triangular rulers for drawing angles), and a compass (a pointed instrument for carving your name in the desk). These items would then spend the rest of the child's school career jumbled up and partially unserviceable in the depths of their pencil case.

Scissors are as old as paper. Although scissor-type implements have been found dating to prior epochs, it was the Ancient Egyptians who first produced them consistently, and from then on scissors have been a key

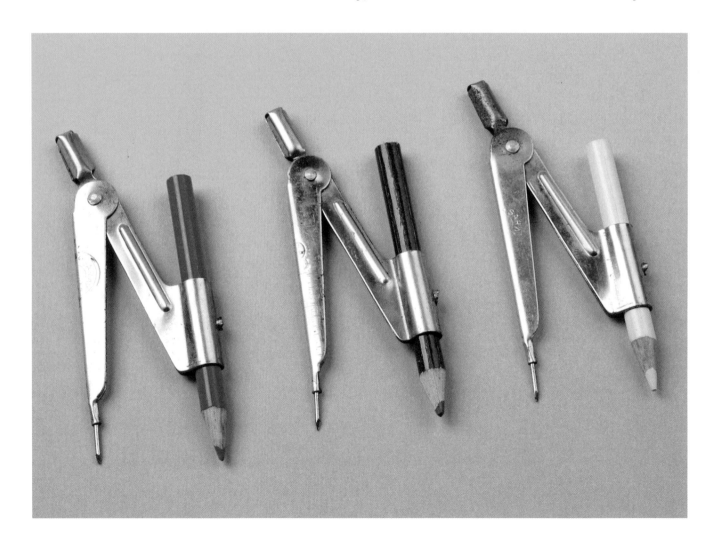

CRAYOLA

There is a very pretty Wikipedia page which features a swatch of each one of the more than 200 types of crayon that Crayola has produced since they set up shop in 1903. These include every imaginable hue, as well as metallic, glittery, glow in the dark, fluorescent and even scented crayons. So diverse and successful are Crayola crayons that there can be few people who are not transported back to their youth by the sight of that unmistakable wrapper, combined with that unmistakable, oily aroma.

In Europe, early childhood education started to be a thing in the early 1800s (the word kindergarten was coined in 1840 by German educator Friedrich Fröbel), while it took a few more decades to catch on in the US (the first official kindergarten was opened there in 1868). Artistic activities were considered from the out-set to be an integral part of development, but the widely available art supplies were of course unsuited to infants. This provoked a massive expansion of production of wax crayons to cater to the new market, and at one point 300 companies were selling one variant or another. The major problem, however, was that most of the pigments used to make them were highly toxic, and small children love chewing things.

Although they started out providing the colours for car tyres, it was the New York-based Binney and Smith Company who came up with the breakthrough when they developed non-toxic pigments and launched them as Crayola brand crayons. The name came from Mrs. Binney herself, and is a combination of the French for chalk, *craie*, with the first syllable of that lovely word 'oleaginous', in reference to the wax used to make the crayons. The fact that the eight colours they originally sold has blossomed into the myriad shades detailed on Wikipedia is a testament to the unshowy excellence of the Crayola product.

Above: period Crayola advertising

Below: a package of Crayola crayons from the early stages of the company's existence

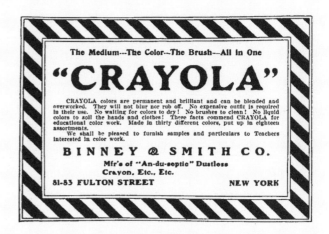

Above: some vintage classroom supplies from around the world, from the selection at Inkwell Berlin

feature of any stationery set, as well as an opportunity to produce dazzlingly elaborate designs. It was not until the Eighteenth Century, however, that the modern pivoted scissor took off, when in 1761 a Mr. Robert Hinchliffe hung a sign outside his house in Cheney Square, London, that read 'fine scissor manufacturer'.

Consider the abacus. An ancient calculating system, beautiful in its simplicity, it consists a series of wires strung with wooden beads that can be used to model numbers up to 9,999,999,999. A common feature in western classrooms up to around the turn of the last century, it was superseded by a rather fascinating device that has since become extinct in its turn: the slide rule.

The most basic slide rules use two logarithmic scales to enable the user to quickly and easily multiply or divide numbers, and more complex models enable other calculations, such as square roots or trigonometric functions; a nautical

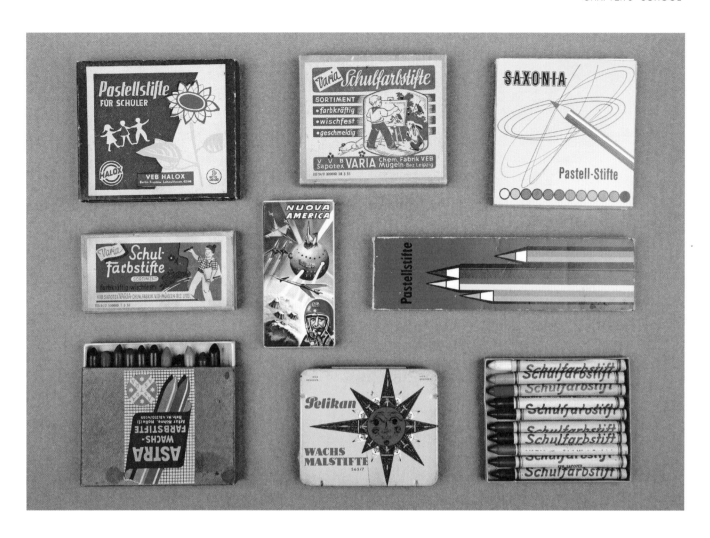

Above: a selection of period colouring instrument in the original packaging

Below: a slide rule, once the *sine qua non* of the engineer's craft

slide rule invented in 1845 could even be used to determine the rising and setting of the sun and important stars.

For decades, engineers carried a slide rule the way gunslingers carried their pistols, and with comparable bravura. The development of affordable personal calculators, however, all but did away with them (the SIN, COS and TAN buttons substitute functions that were performed on a slide rule). While the calculator is quicker and more reliable, some parties inevitably rued the decline of the hands-on approach the slide rule promoted. Very few schoolchildren did, though.

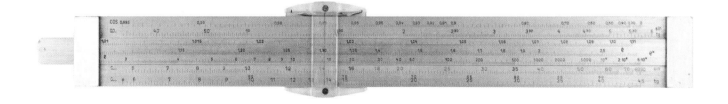

FELT-TIP PEN
AND HIGHLITER

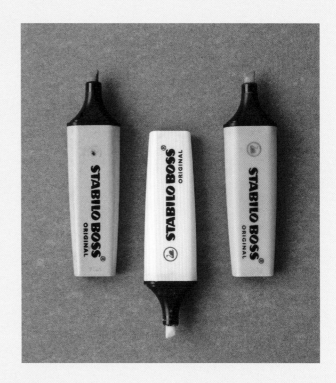

The felt-tip pen was the creation of Japanese inventor Yukio Horie. Yukio was founder of the Dai Nippon Bungu Co., and his fibre-tip Pentel Pen — *Time* magazine's product of the year in 1963 — eventually ended up bestowing on the company the name it bears today.

Felt pen tech shook up the ink scene, and soon all the big names (Parker, Sheaffer, etc.) were working on their own line. And then one smaller company, Carter's Ink, came up with the twist that was to result in the birth of the highlighter as we know it today: yellow.

As some ad copy for the first Carter Hi-Liter pen puts it: 'Clear, "read-through" brilliant yellow lights up words, sentences, paragraphs, telephone numbers, anything. "Hi-lite" them so you can find them again fast!' Those exclamation marks give a taste of how revolutionary the Hi-Liter must have seemed, and there is no doubt that, as *Adventures in Stationery* author James Ward puts it, the pen 'introduced a new way of note taking, a new way of revising, a new way of studying'.

Just as with Yukio Horie's Pentel, in the Hi-Liter, capillary action sucked ink through a filter when the tip was pressed to the paper, enabling an even, fluid application. The water-based ink also dried instantly, and did not saturate the paper as alcohol-based ink might. And Carter's Hi-Liter remains a highly popular pen in the US under its name of Sharpie (which is in fact almost a genericized trademark).

In 1971, the German Schwan Pencil Factory began to produce a similar type of highlighter called the Stabilo Boss, a name that has been synonymous with highlighting for generations of European schoolchildren. The pen is notable for its flat, chunky shape, very easy on the hand, and its tip, which is cut in such as way as to allow for different widths of line, so one can simply underline, or highlight the entire line of text: a deeply elegant design feature. Stabilo is today the world's biggest single producer of highlighters.

And even in the digital world, highlighting remains a widespread feature: word processing programs allow you to highlight (in the classic fluorescent ink colour), as do e-books and PDFs. Some websites even show up the 'most highlighted' section in an article, showing how deeply the highlighter has penetrated into our culture of reading and studying.

It was in the 1970s that pocket calculators first became widely available, and remained a feature of schoolbags for a long time. Progression up the grades was marked by an increase in the sophistication of the calculator you were required to have, culminating in the scientific calculator with its range of buttons offering algebraic functions. But calculators are on the way out, along with many items of school supplies once considered essential, in the face of the ubiquity of the digital device. The electronic tablet features programs for taking notes, for drawing and colouring, for writing homework; they provide easy access via the web to incredibly sophisticated calculators, as well as dictionaries and Wikipedia. They can also be used to access e-books that can be highlighted (but not covered with graffiti for the titillation of future generations).

Top: an example of the Hewlett-Packard HP-35, one of the first scientific hand-held electronic calculators

Bottom: period advertising for the HP-35

MUSEO DEL QUADERNO

Enzo Bottura's passion for antique school notebooks was first sparked when he stumbled across a cache while searching for material on aeronautics in 2001. Tommaso Pollio's collection, meanwhile, stems from the moment when a friend gave him six as a present. The two ended up meeting online in 2012 and embarked together on a four-year-long search round all Italy, building up a collection of over 8,000 different notebooks.

Italy has the most venerable and most vibrant tradition of school notebooks in the world. For more than a century, a notebook with an elaborate and gorgeously illustrated cover was an essential feature of every child's schoolbag. Bottura and Pollio's project, the Museo del Quaderno, is dedicated to '*tutta la sublime poesia*' of this astonishing culture, and their archive now consists of approximately 40,000 images of notebook covers.

Aside from being gems of illustration and design, each one presents a compressed vision of contemporary Italy.

Many of them clearly fulfil a propaganda function, their makers having realized that these notebooks entered 100% of Italian households, and were thus the ideal medium to contribute to the cementing of the nascent nation state, and introducing a sense of civic unity in among Italy's disparate peoples. We can trace their origin to the 'Coppino' law of 1877, which made education compulsory for children between the ages of 6 and 9.

From that moment on, the notebooks faithfully mirrored contemporary artistic styles, historical events, and social and educational mores, all in a visual style that was both appealing and comprehensible to the largely rural population. In addition, within their covers the notebooks featured much diverse information, from multiplication tables to facts and data as well as handy lifestyle tips, to the extent that they have been called encyclopaedias for the poor.

Museo de Quaderno is soon to publish a book featuring covers by 600 different artists, a testament to this unique and glorious tradition that, like so much else, was dealt a death blow by the increased industrialization of the stationery industry in the second part of the Twentieth Century: the final section of the Museo's online archive, for the years 1970-1980, contains only six notebooks.

Opposite page and above: a selection of covers from the voluminous collection of the Museo del Quaderno

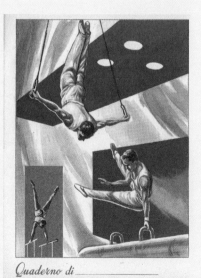

KAKIMORI

SHOP, STATIONERY

Tokyo	Japan

The aim of Tokyo's awesome Kakimori is 'to re-evaluate the importance of writing'. One of their most popular products is the customized notebook — this is a service which enables customers to combine different elements to make up their own bespoke notebook, which is then assembled before their eyes. And, as Akio Toda explains here on behalf of owner Takuma Hirose, complementing their beautiful range of fountain pens there is the 'Ink Stand', at which customers may design their own fountain pen ink.

"In the modern era, technology is quickly replacing old ways of doing things. We even have daily conversations via electronic devices. People may think using pen and paper is too old-fashioned for this generation.

However, we strongly believe that writing is still important for thinking, creating ideas, and communicating with other people. That is why at Kakimori our goal is to give people the opportunity to realize once again the importance of writing.

Digital devices have come to replace traditional stationery. We cannot stop this technological shift. Thus we first need to accept and understand this shift, and then provide stationery based on our understanding.

Previous and current spread: a wide selection of paper and paper-related products are beautifully displayed at Kakimori

For example, nowadays we have fewer opportunities to write by hand, due to technological change. Thus the value and importance of writing by hand have become greater than before. This is the reason we sell customized notebooks and original fountain pen inks at our store. In fact, our customized notebooks are our biggest seller.

Another example of this is letter writing. Would you prefer to receive a love letter via SMS, or handwritten on attractive paper? I believe most people prefer the paper letter. Do you ever look back over your text messages after years have passed? Smart phones are good for daily communication, but physical letters are better for special purposes. I also believe that stationery shops should emphasise the value and importance of physical letters.

This philosophy is also expressed in our Kakimori case-bound notebook. We would like customers to use this notebook when they want to write something important, and to keep it on their bookshelf. Then, when they want to turn back to the past after many years, they can recapture the feeling they had at that moment. This notebook is universal, simple, and its manufacturing process is very traditional; we select fine paper for the inside and fabric for the cover.

Another popular piece is the Tetzbo brass ball-point pen. Its form is very neat and beautifully simple, and you can really appreciate its craftsmanship.

At Kakimori, we select products with reasonable prices. We do not offer 'luxury' products because we would like customers to use these products on a daily basis. Much of our inspiration is based on daily communication with customers at the store, and we try to have a little chat with each one, to find out what they are looking for. We have no one specific customer: we welcome customers who share our concept, come in to our store and become fans!

Nevertheless, our website is the most important tool to educate customers about our core concepts. Most customers who come to our store have discovered our website first. We consider the website to be our commercial marketing tool, and a large proportion of our income comes via this route.

Even though our daily lives are full of digital devices, we believe people appreciate the value of old-fashioned style. A few years ago, it was said that everything around us would soon be converted to a digital format. However, we think people have come to realize the value of a balance between digital and analogue."

RAD AND HUNGRY	
ONLINE SHOP	
Seattle	U.S.A.

Rad and Hungry provide a unique and truly radical service. Each month the team travel somewhere in the world and then send their subscribers a Something Mighty (STMT) stationery box, featuring a kit of office supplies sourced locally from that month's country. The concept sprung from founder Hen Chung's equal passions for travel and office supplies, and has blossomed into a cult, online-only stationery sensation.

"At Rad and Hungry, we believe in getting to know people and places through commerce and design. Someone else's daily diet of lo-fi goods is simple to her yet sacred to us, and vice versa. We're taken by the concept that simple, daily items are given new meaning through travel. It transforms the everyday into something inspired, connecting far-flung groups of people who love style, travel and design.

Our typical customer works in the creative industry. We have a mix of graphic designers, architects, engineers, creative directors and other professionals who still draw and sketch on a daily basis with paper and a pen or pencil. But we also have customers who don't fit that audience. What surprised us (but totally makes sense) was the number of attorneys who sign up for our subscription boxes. Attorneys are another group that still use pencil and paper on a daily basis.

Previous and current spread: Rad and Hungry stands out for its quirky and eye-catching selections of products from around the world

Our perfect customer? Someone like us. Someone who appreciates simple, daily-diet design. They see beauty and value in things that are super simple and mundane — the stuff that's often overlooked and forgotten. They're people that aren't searching for the most expensive or best-quality goods. Instead, they appreciate the simple-but-stylish basics in their daily routine because they choose to be conscious of the things that surround them.

This is our fifth year and we've slowly started to expand our selection of goods. For example, we stock a keyring hook that also functions as a clip for hanging artwork. We stock a really cool zine. Both items were sourced during a trip to Brazil — both have a story that resonated with us, and so we felt they were a good fit for our shop.

Our inspiration comes from travel. Every month we visit a different country to hunt down stationery and office supplies. We search for the most basic supplies — the stuff the average student or office worker uses. A key requirement for our

selection is that the goods are still locally made — or, at minimum, designed by a local company. We also focus heavily on products that have a long history. We search for companies that have been around forever, cranking out the same rad products with very little design changes from the original.

I might explain the lasting allure of stationery in terms of the fact that, while smart phones and computers can be great for automating tasks and can save time when performing certain tasks, nothing beats writing a to-do list on paper. It's tangible, it's more satisfying to write down a list and then physically cross off the completed task. It's like giving yourself a hi-five!

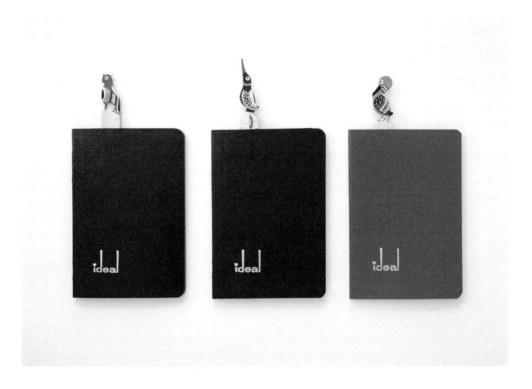

I also think daily journals keep stationery relevant. The connection you have when you physically write down a daily record of things you experienced, people you're grateful for, dreams, whatever — when you actually write that down, it's deeper than when you throw down words madly typing on a computer.

Our biggest sellers are all of our fountain pens and related items, vintage pencils, and our monthly subscription boxes.

Rad and Hungry was born out of my love of collecting office supplies. I think everyone probably has a weakness. For me? I can't part with really old vintage pencils and vintage notebooks. The typography on both is almost always rad, and I love how they give a glimpse of graphic design from years past.

My favourite item has to be the goldenrod pencil. It perfectly represents lo-fi, daily-diet design. It's a workhorse, but overlooked because it's so ordinary. People have gotten so familiar with goldenrod pencils that one never stands out. But we notice. We know they're important. Big things can happen from something as simple as putting pencil to paper.

Charming, vintage school notebooks
from a variety of countries

Some extremely hot French Reynolds
fountain pens from the 1980s

Ever since our first sourcing trip to Mexico back in 2010,
we've been obsessing over Mirado pencils. They're the ultimate
everyday pencil with mad history. The Mirado is a descendant
of the Eagle Mikado of pre-World War II times. We love that
the Mirado pencil has a history that runs deep, and we're
constantly searching them out to add to our collection.

We found a large stash of vintage French fountain pens from the
'80s during a trip to Italy. I'd never come across the models we
found and had to research the company. The fountain pens are so
perfectly 80s and we even scored the original display cases.

The recent surge of attention to stationery totally makes sense
to me. It feels like a natural reaction to how tech-heavy our
lives have become. People react by wanting the opposite. This
whole 'slow movement' has become a trend. I think that people's
interest in stationery is beautiful. I think it's about people
connecting with time. And when people discover stationery
ephemera from years past, it's like discovering someone else's
history. You get a first-hand experience of a stranger's life...
you get to discover design from another era, you can map out
things from their day, you get to see and touch history."

CHAPTER N°9

OFFICE

———

The cornucopia of the stationery cupboard

The 'secret beating heart' of any office, according to writer Jenny Diski, is the stationery cupboard, with its 'floor-to-ceiling shelves laden with neat stacks of packets, piles and boxes, lined up, tidy, everything patiently waiting for you to take one from the top, or open the lid and grab a handful... A cornucopia of everything you would never run out of.' Although the office stationery cupboard doesn't differ much from that of the school, what changes is that now we have free, unrestricted access, and can range among its shelves to our hearts' desire. The days of safety scissors are behind us.

Previous spread, image courtesy Present & Correct

Below, top: an old Strip Paper Fastener, probably produced in Germany circa 1910

Below, bottom: a flock of staplers

According to some accounts, the first staples were made of gold and bedecked with precious stones. This touch would indeed have been in keeping with the milieu in which the first stapler was used, the court of Louis XV of France, where the increasing reliance on paper as a tool of government had created a need for a device that would keep individual sheets together. It was only in the 1800s, however, that this need became sufficiently widespread among the general populace as to provoke the massification of the stapler.

Although several names have been held up as the godfather of the modern stapler, it seems the real pioneer was American George McGill, who invented both a small bendable brass fastener and a machine for sticking it into paper, showcasing the combination at an industrial fair in 1876. And in 1879, McGill launched his Patent Single Stroke Staple Press, the first commercially successful stapler.

Weighing more than a kilogram, the device is an attractive bit of early industrial design, featuring a cast iron base and an arm on a pivot with a spring-loaded plunger. The trick

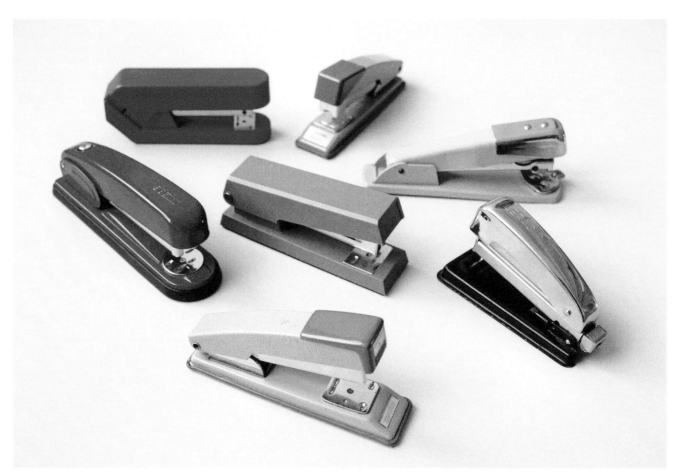

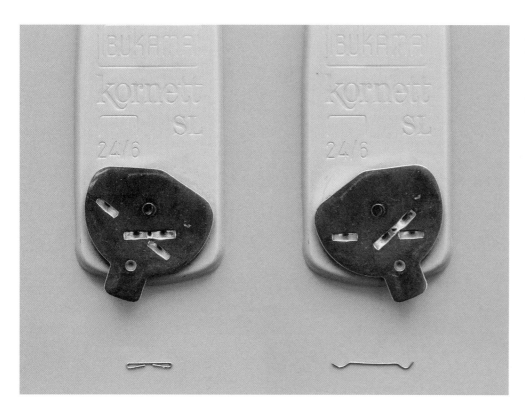

On the left, the anvil position allows for the staple to be bent inward; on the right, the staple is bent outwards, making it easier to unfaste the sheets

Below: a selection of staples from different eras, all in their original packaging

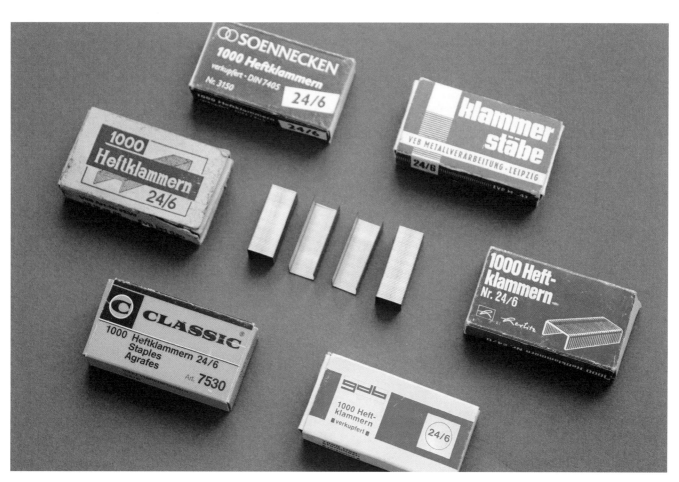

is that the base is shaped to bend the points of the staple inward after they'd gone through the paper, much as today's staplers do. The 'single stroke' part of the name comes from the fact that the machine needed only one movement to insert the stapler into the paper and bend round its ends — most other staplers at the time required a second, usually manual, step. Various tweaks and additions were made on this design — most of them to do with the number of staples that could be inserted in one go, as the single speed could only hold one staple at a time — but it was not until 1941 that the stapler as we know it today made its appearance, in the form of the 'four way paper stapler'.

Today millions of dollars are spent annually on staplers around the world. It seems, however, that very few of their countless users know about one of the functions of the modern stapler. Have one to hand? Pull back the top half, as if you were going to use it to tack something to a wall. Now, you see the metal base plate? This is called the anvil. Press your finger up underneath it and you will find that it pops up, enabling you to swivel it round and click it back into place. Your stapler is now in the 'sheer' setting (the normal one is called 'reflexive'): this will enable you to staple papers very loosely, in such a way that the staple can easily be removed. Cool, right?

Staplers and hole punches are the great desktop duo, and no upmarket workspace would be complete without one of each

DESTAPLER

The destapler or staple remover was first patented by William G. Pankonin of Chicago, Illinois, in 1936 (although it is based on a device to unpick stitching, invented by Irish seamstress Meghan Rooney). It is composed of two jaws that work together in a sort of pincer motion to unfold and remove the staple in one action. The destapler is distinguished as being the most evil-looking stationery item ever created.

ZENITH 548

The Zenith's name was not idly chosen — it truly represents a high point and benchmark in stapler design. With its form vaguely reminiscent of Moby Dick, each Zenith 548 features nickel-plated brass parts and lead-free enamel paint, and comes with a lifetime guarantee. Its deep-set fulcrum enables it to staple together more sheets at one time than any other commercial stapler. Launched in 1924 by Balma, Capoduri & C., in 1954 it was nominated for the Compasso d'Oro, the most prestigious Italian industrial design prize.

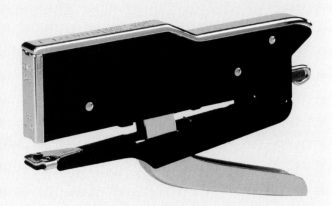

A Zenith 548 on top of its orignal patent

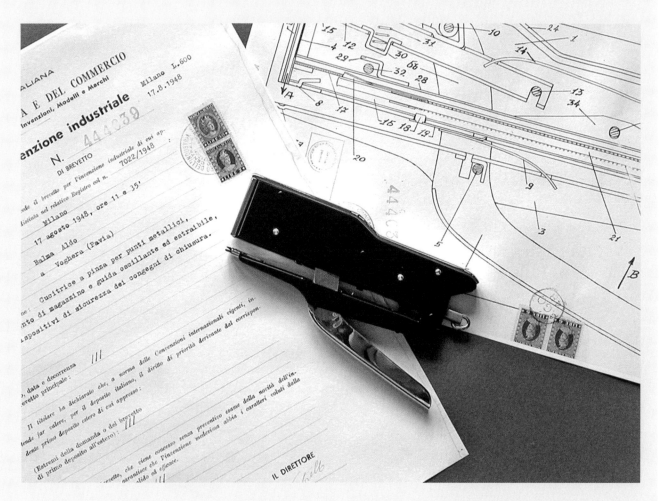

A selection of hole punches from different stages in this object's evolution

A two-hole punch produced by F.Soennecken model nr.237

in the same colours and finish, sometimes accompanied by a tape dispenser of the same clan. The squat, amphibian form of the hole punch has remained fairly consistent for decades, and seems to have emerged more or less fully formed, in one of those interesting migrations that sometimes occur in engineering: the basic form and mechanism of the hole punch were already in wide use, and all it took was for someone to adapt them.

In 1893, Charles Brooks of New Jersey patented a device for punching holes in paper. Although he intended it for use by ticket inspectors on public transport, its built-in receptacle for collecting the punched-out paper circles made it functionaly identical to the modern hole punch. Then in 1885, John Laney from Indiana patented a two-hole punch, this time explicitly designed for paper storage. It seems that people were working on the concept on both sides of the Atlantic, for in 1886 the German stationery inventor Friedrich Soennecken filed a patent for his Papierlocher für Sammelmappen hole punch: it's beautiful. (Friedrich

Reinforcers for punched sheets in
original West German packaging

Nietzche, incidentally, is on record as being a fan of the
Soennecken fountain pen.)

The sole function of the hole punch is, of course, to punch
holes in paper, generally so they can be kept in files and ring
binders. Just as there are different types of file, so there are
different types of hole punch. The universal ISO standard
specifies two holes with a diameter of 6±0.5 mm, their
centres 80±0.5 mm from each other and 12±1 mm from the
edge of the paper. But then there are three- and four-hole
hole punches, and all the usual confusion vis-a-vis the USA's
stubborn refusal to embrace the simple elegance of metric
measurements (not to mention Sweden's wacky 'triohålning'
system). The small circles of paper that are removed by the
hole punch are known as chads, as are the circles of paper
punched out of ballots in Votomatic polling booths in the US.
The controversy surrounding the 2000 presidential elections
led to these machines being phased out, but not before
bringing into circulation that memorable bit of jargon,
the hanging chad.

But there are those who choose to forego entirely the hole
punch, and keep their papers in order using that immortal
piece of office stationery, the paper clip. The Early Office

ROLODEX

There was a time when everyone had address books, al-
phabetized notebooks in which one would accumulate
telephone numbers and addresses, crossing them out
only when the person they pertained to moved away,
dumped you, or died. In the world of business, however,
the must-have contacts organizer was the Rolodex.

As the name, a portmanteau word of 'rolling' and 'index', hints, the Rolodex is a set of index cards on a rotating
spindle, enabling contact info to be found at the merest
touch of a finger. First launched in 1956, the Rolodex is
fighting a rearguard action against digital address books,
but retains a degree of retro charm.

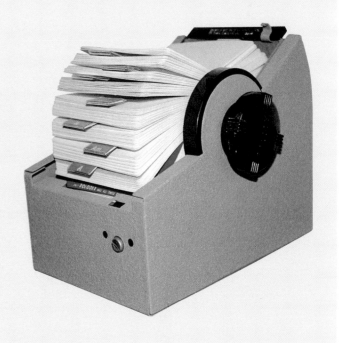

Museum shows that the paper clip was in a certain sense invented in 1867 by Samuel B. Fay. Over the following 30 years, however, over 50 other designs were patented; in the words of Henry Petroski, 'few products have been more formed, de-formed, and re-formed than the common paper clip', and there is a fascinating and ingenious range of designs that preceded the appearance of the recognizably modern paper clip, among them the Owl, the Banjo, the Eureka, the Simplex, the Perfection, and the Common Sense, each one more elaborate than the last, some of them almost like Celtic runes.

The 'modern' paper clip, the design that came to eclipse all these others, was in fact a model that emerged fully-formed rather than evolving over time. Known as the Gem, one of the first illustrations we have of it dates to April 1899, when Connecticut native William Middlebrook applied for a patent for a 'machine for making paper clips'. Along with

An assorment of clips and paper clips;
image courtesy Present & Correct

THE RUBBER BAND

———

That staple of classroom warfare the rubber band was first patented on March 17, 1845, by Stephen Perry, a British inventor and founder of Messers Perry and Co, Rubber Manufacturers of London, pioneers in early vulcanized rubber products. But it was William Spencer of Alliance, Ohio, who made the rubber band a household item.

An employee of the Pennsylvania Railroad, he had access to offcut rubber pieces which he used to experiment. Success ensued, and he opened his second factory in 1944, in 1957 patenting the Alliance rubber band, which came to set the standard for rubber bands. Alliance Rubber is today the world's biggest rubber band manufacturer, producing more than 14 million of them each year.

the diagrams of the machine was included an illustration of a Gem, in exactly the proportions familiar to us today. And what proportions! As Owen Edwards wrote in his book *Elegant Solutions*, '[I]f all that survives of our fatally flawed civilization is the humble paper clip, archaeologists from some galaxy far, far away may give us more credit than we deserve. In our vast catalogue of material innovation, no more perfectly conceived object exists.'

There is no doubt that the Gem paper clip is a masterpiece of stationery design — its form is its function, and vice versa, with not a single millimetre of bent steel too many, or too few. The Gem is also a symbol of a how a lot (of design, technology, economics) can be compressed into a little. This is a fact that was not lost on the great economist Adam Smith, who saw in the pin, the paper clip's predecessor, the perfect illustration of the benefits to be attained from the division of labour, describing in *The Wealth of Nations* how '[O]ne man draws the wire, another straightens it, a third cuts it, a fourth points it, a fifth grinds the top for

Drawing pins made by Pelikan,
featuring an engraved design

receiving the head.' (It may be hard to conceive of how so
many different hands had to participate in the production
of a humble pin, but such is the nature of even the simplest
of objects.)

Smith's pin didn't change much from the moment he wrote
the book until the middle of the Nineteenth Century when,
like so many other objects, it began to be on the receiving
end of attempts at innovation. The most notable of these
was the drawing pin, or thumbtack as it is known in the
US. There are different theories about who first came up
with the design which we still use today, that of a round
metal button with a sharp pin sticking out of the middle of
it, but it seems we can state with confidence that it was in
use by the mid-1800s (and was thus not invented by German
watchmaker Johann Kirsten, although it may have been his
design that was first mass-produced).

Another spin on the pin constitutes a 'short steel spike
embedded in a miniature top hat', to deploy James Ward's
succinct description, generally known as a pushpin.

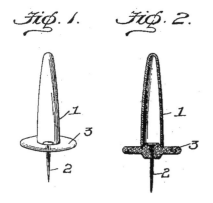

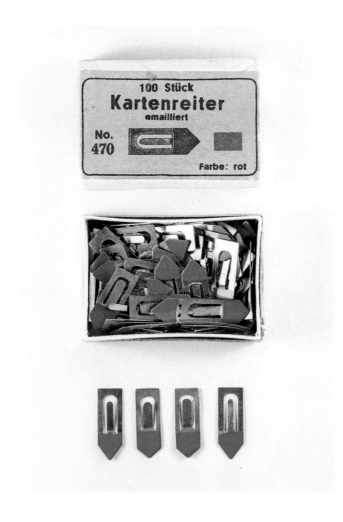

These were invented by an Edwin Moore, who in 1900 was working in a New Jersey photo lab. When hanging up prints to dry, he found that the drawing pin obliged him to bring his fingertips into contact with the paper, leaving a mark. His solution seems simple in retrospect but was revolutionary enough to take the stationery world by storm, and the firm he set up off the back of its success, the Moore Push-Pin Company, remains a big name in the production of 'little things'.

Jenny Diski concludes her meditation on offices and the little things that stock them, quoted at the beginning of this chapter, with a reflection on the demise of the workplaces she knew as a young worker. As more and more firms outsource what used to be internal positions, creating a generation of freelancers who do the same work for less money and none of the benefits or security, it seems that the days of office stationery may be slipping away. 'I suspect,' Diski ruefully concludes, 'that the sumptuous stationery cupboard is getting to be as rare as a monthly salary cheque'.

Push Pin. The original drawings from the patent granted to Moore in 1900

Below left: East German-made indexing tags
Below right: Milton page fasteners

DAPHNA LAURENS

DESIGNER, CLIPS

Eindhoven	Nederlands

Studio Daphna Laurens is a leading contemporary Dutch design atelier. The studio's approach revolves around giving everyday objects a new incarnation. The pieces they create fuse function and expression, casting a new light on often overlooked arti-facts. Part of the cutting-edge Dutch Invertuals collective, they have exhibited all over Europe.

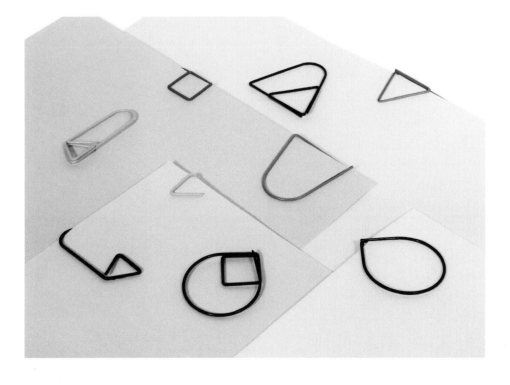

It's been over a century since any designer has tried to get to grips with the paper clip. This has meant that the classic 'gem' design has come to be interchangeable with the paper clip itself. Studio Daphna Laurens is a project of two graduates of the Eindhoven Design Academy, Daphna Isaacs Burggraaf and Laurens Manders. Their clip series is one of few examples of contemporary efforts to reinvent the wheel of the gem paper clip, and their designs showcase the unexpected range of expressive possibilities offered by this most unpretentious of stationery items.

The designers follow a shape-driven philosophy. Their clips started life as simple line drawings with no utilitarian function. Transformed into bent spring steel shapes, they acquire both grace and utility, and come to embody many key values of industrial design. Colorful, playful, functional, the Daphna Laurens paper clips transform a sheaf of paper into a canvas.

The final designs of the Daphna Laurens paper clip project

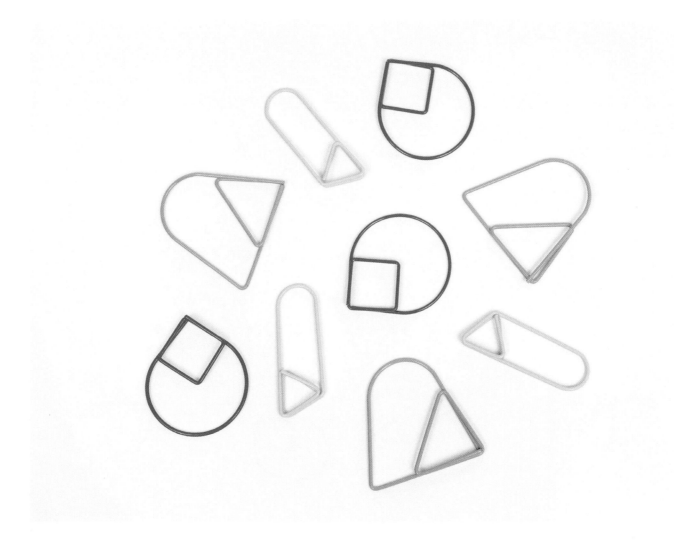

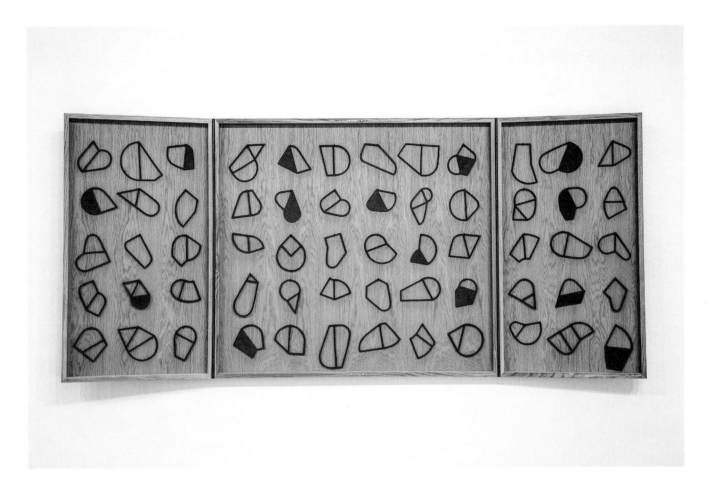

A display of the prototypes

PHOTO CREDITS

Andrea Kroth: 38, 40, 41, 42 bottom
Baron Fig: 119
Balma, Capoduri & C.: 145, 195
Bic: 101
Bonvini: 158, 160, 161, 162, 163
Brevi Manu: 121
Conté: 13
Christof Zollinger: 98, 99, 103
Daniela Luccherini: 123 bottom
Daphna Laurens: 202, 203, 204, 205
Erasable Podcast: 35, 36, 37
Eskesen: 100
Faber: 124, 126, 127
Faber-Castell: 12
Field Notes: 116 top
Gunther Schmidt: 49 top, 51
Leuchtturm1917: 119
HP Virtual Museum: 177
Internoitaliano: 30, 32, 33
Isabella Paleari: 123 top
Kakimori: 180, 182, 183
Jaime Narvaez: 116 bottom
Liz Seabrook: 80, 82, 83, 84
Luca Bogoni: 8, 15, 16, 17, 21, 34, 46, 47, 48, 49 bottom, 50, 52, 54, 55, 79, 92, 95 right, 114, 140, 150, 152, 153, 154, 155, 156, 157 top, 174, 175, 192, 193, 194, 199
Maria Silvano: 18, 19, 60, 62, 63, 64, 65, 72, 95 top, 168, 171, 172, 196, 197, 200, 201 top

Martin Z. Schröder: 157
Maurizio Bendandi: 77, 78, 79, 95 bottom, 96, 97, 144
MT Masking Tape: 146, 148, 149
Museo del Quaderno: 178, 179
Nakajima Jukyudo: 44, 56, 58, 59
Octaevo: 120
Papier Tigre: 66, 68, 69
Papelote: 134, 136, 137, 138, 139
Pascal Rohé: 42 top
Pen Store: 104, 106, 107
Present & Correct: 6, 70, 73, 74, 76, 108, 110, 111, 112, 113, 190, 198
Publicaçoes Serrote: 128, 130, 131, 132, 133
Numisantica: 10
Rob Lavinsky: 11
McNally Jackson: 86, 88, 89, 90, 91
Moleskine: 123
Nicholas Delauney: 13
Rad and Hungry: 184, 186, 187, 188, 189
Ryan Segedi: 26, 27, 28, 29
Savignac: 101
Sean Malone: 22
Sergio Ramazzotti: 122
Storage.it: 118 bottom
Suck UK: 121 bottom
Tampographe Sardon: 164, 165, 166, 167
UI Stencils: 118 top
Write Sketch &: 117

IMAGES COURTESY OF

Balma, Capoduri & C - www.zenithbc.com
Baron Fig - www.baronfig.com
Belleza Infinita - www.bellezainfinita.com
Bic - www.bicworld.com
Blackwingpages (Sean Malone) - www.blackwingpages.com
Bonvini - bonvini1909.com
Brevi Manu - www.brevimanu.de
Choosing Keeping - www.choosingkeeping.com
Crayola - www.crayola.com
CW Pencils Enterprise - www.cwpencils.com
Daphna Laurens - www.daphnalaurens.nl
David Rees - www.artisanalpencilsharpening.com
Erasable Podcast - www.erasable.us
Eskesen - www.eskesen.com
Faber - www.faber-nb.it
Faber-Castell - www.faber-castell.de
Field Notes - www.fieldnotesbrand.com
Fisher Space Pen - www.spacepen.com
Giulio Iacchetti - www.giulioiacchetti.com
HP Virtual Museum - www.hp.com
Inkwell Berlin - www.inkwellberlin.com
Internoitaliano - www.internoitaliano.com
Jaime Narvaez - www.jaimenarvaez.com
Kakimori - www.kakimori.com

Leuchtturm1917 - www.leuchtturm1917.de
Lexikaliker (Gunther Schmidt) - www.lexikaliker.de
Martin Z. Schröder - www.druckerey.de
McNally Jackson - www.mcnallyjacksonstore.com
Moleskine - www.moleskine.com
MT Masking Tape - www.mt-maskingtape.com
Museo del Quaderno - www.museodelquaderno.it
Nakajima Jukyudo - www.njk-brand.co.jp
Numisantica - www.numisantica.com
Octaevo - www.octaevo.com
Orlando Vallucci - www.pergamena.com
Papelote - www.papelote.cz
Papier Tigre - www.papiertigre.fr
Pen Store - www.penstore.se
Present & Correct - www.presentandcorrect.com
Publicaçoes Serrote - www.serrote.com
Rad and Hungry - www.radandhungry.com
Rob Lavinsky - www.irocks.com
R.S.V.P. - www.rsvp-berlin.de
Storage.it - www.storage.it
Suck UK - www.suck.uk.com
Tampographe Sardon - www.le-tampographe-sardon.blogspot.de
UI Stencils - www.uistencils.com
Write Sketch & - www.writesketchand.com

FURTHER READING

Johann Beckmann - *A History of Inventions, Discoveries and Origins* (1797)

Vicki Cobb - *The Secret Life of School Supplies* (J. B. Lippincott, 1981)

William E. Covill - *Ink Bottles and Inkwells* (Sullwold Publishing, 1979)

Floyd L. Darrow - *The Story of an Ancient Art, from the Earliest Adhesives to Vegetable Glue* (Perkins Glue, 1930)

Leonhard Dingwerth - *Kleine Anspitzer-Fibel: Geschichte und Beschreibung historischer Bleistift-Anspitzer* (Verlag Dingwerth, 2008)

Jenny Diski - 'Post-its, push pins, pencils'. *London Review of Books*, 31 July 2014, pp. 3-7.

Owen Edwards and Douglas Whyte - *Elegant solutions: Quintessential Technology for a User-friendly World* (Crown, 1989)

Marco Ferreri - *Pencils* (Corraini, 1996)

Henry Gostony and Stuart Schneider - *The Incredible Ball Point Pen: A Comprehensive History and Price Guide* (Schiffer, 1998)

L. Graham Hogg - *The Biro Ballpoint Pen* (LGH Publications, 2007)

J. P. Lacroux and L. van Cleem - *La mémoire des Sergent Major* (Editions Ramsay/Editions Quintette, 1988)

Cliff Lawrence - *Fountain Pens* (Collector Books, 1977)

Kevin M. Moist and David Banash - *Contemporary Collecting – Objects, Practices and the Fate of Things* (Scarecrow Press 2013)

Henry Petroski - *The Pencil: A History of Design and Circumstance* (Knopf Doubleday, 1989)

Leonard Read - 'I, Pencil: My Family Tree as Told to Leonard E. Read'. *The Freeman*, December 1958.

David Rees - *How to Sharpen Pencils: A Practical & Theoretical Treatise on the Artisanal Craft of Pencil Sharpening for Writers, Artists, Contractors, Flange Turners, Anglesmiths, & Civil Servants* (Melville, 2013)

James Ward - *Adventures in Stationery: A Journey Through Your Pencil Case* (Profile, 2015)

ACKNOWLEDGEMENTS

Meike Wander warned us that trying to classify and categorize the world of stationery would lead us to understand that the ocean cannot be made to fit in a glass. Our first thanks are due to her for putting us on the right track. Ali Gitlow and Prestel believed in the idea that led to this book, while Conor Jack Creighton provided the initial impetus. Meeting collectors like Orlando Vallucci, Tommaso Pollio, Enzo Bottura and the Erasable Podcast team made us realize how deep the well of passion can be. Neal Whittington has inspired us with his magnificent compositions, and the contributions of Christof Zollinger, Gunther Schmidt, Sean Malone, and all the participants has enriched this collection with important information, distilled with passion and dedication. Luca Bogoni deployed great skill in the creative composition; his support has been continuous, and not limited to design. Maria Silvano has contributed constant support and great talent to the process of taking photographs. Finally, thanks goes to the editor and author: Angela Nicoletti who held the threads of this tangled skein together, and John Z. Komurki who, with his talent, has been able to close an ocean inside this little box of information, seasoning it with the pepper of his sagacity and wit.

Luca Bendandi, Vetro Editions

Cover image: © Luca Bogoni

© Prestel Verlag, Munich · London · New York, 2016
A member of Verlagsgruppe Random House GmbH
Neumarkter Strasse 28 · 81673 Munich

A project curated by Vetro Editions, www.vetroeditions.com

Prestel Publishing Ltd.
14-17 Wells Street
London W1T 3PD

Prestel Publishing
900 Broadway, Suite 603
New York, NY 10003

Library of Congress Control Number: 2016935127
A CIP catalogue record for this book is available from the British Library.

Editorial direction: Angela Nicoletti, Vetro Editions
Copyediting: John Z. Komurki
Design and layout: Luca Bogoni
Project supervision: Luca Bendandi, Vetro Editions
Production: Friederike Schirge
Separations: David Burghardt
Printing and binding: DZS, d.o.o., Ljubljana
Paper: Tauro

Verlagsgruppe Random House FSC® N001967
Printed in Slovenia
ISBN 978-3-7913-8272-2
www.prestel.com